Chstmas 1998.

A gli... oun
country ...ttle
corner; enjoy.

Lots of love,
Chs. xx

Let me yet know of you whither you are bound.

No, sooth, sir; my determinate voyage is mere extravagancy.

W S Twelfth Night

Oh, go on then :-

Epic Onwards

Falmouth   Penzance   St Ives

To sea again; to see again.

David Weston

Epic Onwards
Falmouth Penzance St Ives

David Weston Gallery

Mevagissey Cornwall England

Published in November 1995
David Weston Gallery
Mevagissey, Cornwall PL26 6UB
England

ISBN 0 9517290 3 9

Printed by Blackfords of Cornwall
Holmbush, St. Austell PL25 3JL

PENZANCE

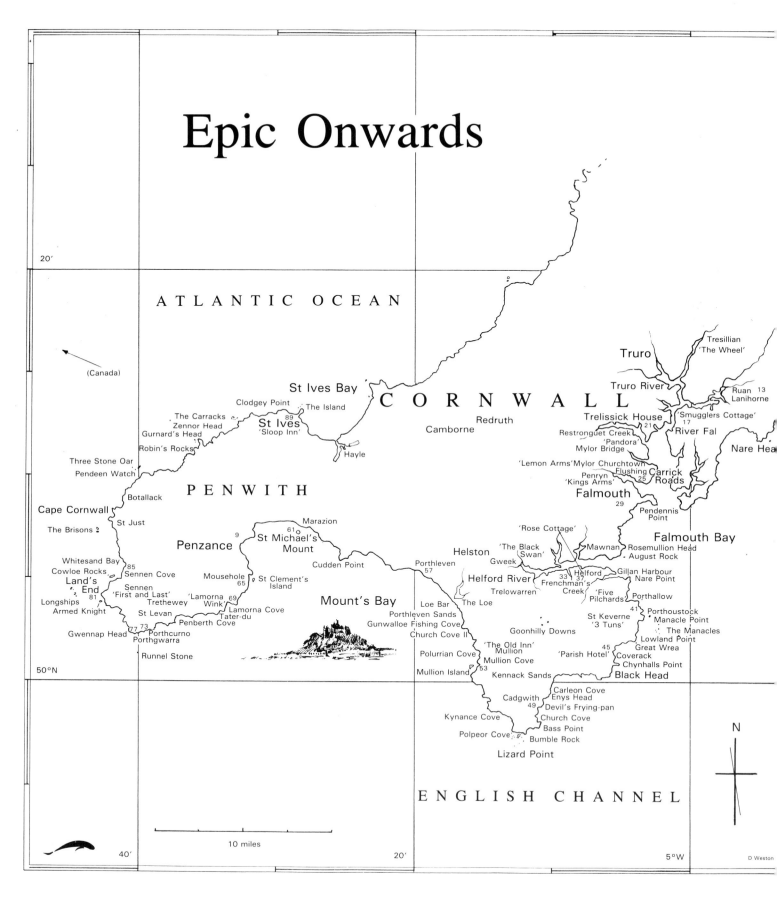

Epic Onwards

ATLANTIC OCEAN

(Canada)

CORNWALL

St Ives Bay

Clodgey Point
The Carracks · St Ives
Zennor Head · 'Sloop Inn'
Gurnard's Head
Robin's Rocks

The Island

Redruth
Camborne

Truro
Tresillian
'The Wheel'

Truro River
Ruan 13
Lanihorne

Trelissick House
Smugglers Cottage'
17
River Fal

Restronguet Creek · 21
'Pandora'
Mylor Bridge
'Lemon Arms'Mylor Churchtown
Penryn · Flushing Carrick
'Kings Arms' · 25 Roads
Nare Hea

Three Stone Oar
Pendeen Watch

Botallack

PENWITH

Marazion
St Michael's
Mount

Cudden Point

'Rose Cottage'

Falmouth
29
Pendennis
Point

Falmouth Bay

Cape Cornwall
St Just

The Brisons 2

Penzance 9
St Clement's
Island

Helston

Porthleven
57

Helford River
Trelowarren

'The Black
Swan'
Gweek
Mawnan Rosemullion Head
August Rock
33 37
Helford
Frenchman's
Creek
Gillan Harbour
Nare Point
'Five
Pilchards'
Porthallow
41

Whitesand Bay 85
Cowloe Rocks Sennen Cove
Land's Mousehole
End 65
81 Sennen
Longships 'First and Last'
Armed Knight Trethewey
St Levan
Gwennap Head 77 73 Porthcurno
Porthgwarra
Runnel Stone

Mount's Bay

Loe Bar
Porthleven Sands
Gunwalloe Fishing Cove
Church Cove II
Polurrian Cove
Mullion Island 53

Goonhilly Downs

St Keverne
'3 Tuns'
45
Coverack

Porthoustock
Manacle Point
The Manacles
Lowland Point
Great Wrea
Chynhalls Point
Black Head

'Lamorna
Wink' 69
Lamorna Cove
Tater-du
Penberth Cove

'The Old Inn'
Mullion
Mullion Cove

'Parish Hotel'

Kennack Sands

Cadgwith
49
Kynance Cove
Polpeor Cove

Carleon Cove
Enys Head
Devil's Frying-pan
Church Cove
Bass Point
Bumble Rock

Lizard Point

ENGLISH CHANNEL

20'

50°N

40'

20'

5°W

10 miles

N

D Weston

Contents

Illustrations

Epic Onwards

Preamble

Half a mile from Ruan Lanihorne a narrow lane runs alongside the little Ruan River. There is an abundance of green and quiet and a riverside lay-by is not all it seems. Twin stone bollards suggest an optional wharf – available when the tide rises above the mud and infiltrates the reedy grasses.

Freshly painted and gleaming brightly white, my old plywood Mirror dinghy, Epic, was tethered to the upstream bollard, ready to be cast off – for my voyage to continue along the South Cornish Coast.

It felt strange raising the mast and attaching the shrouds and fore-stay again. A replay – different tidal river but same date, 5th July. Upstream, immediately to the left of the lay-by/quay, the bank was deeply cushioned with soft lush grass. From that natural slip-way Robin helped me launch the dinghy – soundlessly into still water, watched by a pair of very white swans.

RUAN LANIHORNE

'There is an abundance of green and quiet —'

Realizing there was no food in the offing the swans glided down-stream on a mirror-like surface that reflected clear evening sky. Robin thought he would join them. We set the Blue Bosun (of which more later), fitted the centre-board and rudder, and with a light wind occasionally providing steerage-way he progressed a little way down the creek till it became apparent the tide was turning. He did likewise and rowed back to the lay-by.

The falling river level hastened our loading. With buckets and bags on board, and the sail bundled round the mast, I cast off and exchanged see-you-soons with my middle son. Soon the old Ford was out of sight and the engine sound gradually faded. Silence. I slowly rowed away from Ruan Wharf.

Red Admiral

Robin was nineteen — the age Toby his elder brother was when he ferried me to the Tamar where my odyssey began. Two years on, Robin had transported Epic and me to Ruan Lanihorne — five miles south east of Truro. High (spring) tide was around eight that evening. Butterflies prevented a morning start — not a fear of the 'north five, occasionally six' shipping forecast, but two five feet oil paintings — a tortoiseshell and a red admiral. I had taken and overseen the hanging of my paintings that morning at the Crown Court in Truro. The building preceded, by a few years, the new Tate Gallery in St Ives that had been opened two weeks earlier. The same architects were employed on both projects which were similar in many ways — particularly the hungry-for-paintings, tall white-walled interiors. Judge Taylor, appreciating that the Court was really a gallery where trials for errors (or not) were carried out, set out to enhance the building with works of art.

It was thanks to the *hanging* Judge that my mind was taken away from the continuation of the voyage. The anxious hours when abstract butterflies fluttered were few.

I wondered where Epic was bound. Nostalgia suggested St Ives. In the sixties I spent one long hot summer there – doing a little painting, and in two hotels a lot of washing up. From the kitchen windows of the second hotel I looked down on Porthmeor Beach where the new Tate now stands. A Tateless view of Porthmeor and the Island was the only serious oil painting I took away after an exciting six month sojourn. As a destination St Ives seemed out of the question. Wild water off the Lizard, Land's End and Cape Cornwall was reason enough to suggest a closer terminal.

Amble On

As I neared the River Fal, just a few hundred yards from the wharf, light wafts ruffled the river's surface. In the lee of the hillside along the Ruan River I had been protected from the fresh north wind. I unfurled the Bosun and held the short line Robin had used as a sheet and Epic was soon racing down-stream. A lake about a mile long and half as wide is formed at the tidal limit of the Fal. As I entered the wide, empty stretch of water, a strong gust detached the sheet from the sail. The short sheet Robin had attached I knew was a temporary measure but I should have checked the knot was not. The hectic few minutes taken to restrain the thrashing fabric – wrapping it round the mast and fixing a longer sheet, not only tested my new Bosun but shook me from my reverie. With two turns round the mast, reducing the area of the sail by two thirds, I carried on.

The lake was draining rapidly. Epic was in a backwater to the left of the main channel. I headed for deeper water where the river narrowed and commenced negotiating a one hundred and eighty degree bend to the left. Progress seemed slow. It was slow. The centre-board had gradually buried itself in soft mud and trapped Epic. Not wishing to be stopped so soon, or to test the depth of mud with my new green wellies with their pristine soft linings, I frantically heaved out the muddy board and quickly set to with the oars – digging them in the mud to force Epic through two inches of receding water. Mission accomplished, I let Epic drift to the outer edge of the river – out of the wind in the protection of a high wooded bank. Dead trees, partly submerged and lichened light grey/green, formed obstructions now and then. At one, I carefully looped the painter over a brittle branch allowing Epic to come to rest. I stowed the gear and made the little boat ship-shape.

Cut off from all outside pressures I was happily adrift. My responsibilities for the time being were within arm's reach — mind-time to spare — to reminisce. The launch site was a trigger. The full river invading the grassy margins reminded me of a time when I was eleven. Armed with a newly acquired tank aerial (as in military) fishing rod I was on my first solo sortie to the mighty Severn — which was heavily in flood. I pulled from the brown cloudy water, where cows had grazed a few days before, a monstrous fish. The thrill of the invisible power bending my aerial into a tight curve is a precious memory. My chub in reality weighed only a pound — a leviathan to me at the time when compared to the bullheads and minnows previously taken on stick and thread from a brook nearer home. In the following few years I made weightier conquests — when flies were flicked low under branches, tempting wary brown trout. The incongruous happening — grass *carrying on being grass* despite disappearing under water, still brings back that pleasant early recollection.

Totally unwound and without schedule I wondered whether to spend the night hitched to the branch or carry on down to the Smugglers' Cottage. I wanted to take my time, to slowly adjust to a floating life again. A tingling impatience suggested a compromise. There was an hour or more of daylight left so I opted for a lazy, tide assisted row down to the Smugglers' at Tolverne — three miles away. Just before reaching the restaurant I passed the Truro River junction and began to trace in reverse my track taken two years before. I was heading seaward again — starting another adventure. I tied Epic to the pontoon, entered the Inn and enjoyed a bowl of minestrone and a nightcap pint. It all felt very familiar. The new beginning induced a similar high to the previous ending. Had two years really passed since I cruised those peaceful waterways between sumptuous wooded banks?

SMUGGLERS' COTTAGE

'—I opted for a lazy, tide assisted row down to the Smugglers at Tolverne —'

Preparations

At the end of the last voyage I headed upstream from the Smugglers' and Epic was finally taken from the water at Truro. After being laid up for two winters and a summer she was in need of a service and a few additions. When cleaning the bottom, in preparation for painting, I noticed cracks where the plywood panels almost met. After a trip to a local Do It Yourself store, I did, and became a second class glass-fibre repair exponent. The kit consisted of two square feet or so of very coarse glass mat, a tin of sticky resin and a small tube of hardener, a mixing beaker, brush and *volcanic* sandpaper. Having cleaned round the wounds I prepared my first mix. Within minutes my equipment was depleted disproportionately to results. The hard hot lump of resin that claimed my beaker also encapsulated the brush. Having mastered the critical mixture proportions, manufactured disposable brushes from a broom and acquired a quantity of foil take-away containers, I administered patches, rendering the hull sound. When rubbed down and painted the textural quality of my surgery was surprisingly acceptable. I turned Epic over and carried out more treatment. Some of the glass edging seams had come adrift. The most needy areas I repaired, resisting the temptation to lift lesser suspect sections with my itchy fingernail.

To make sleeping on *board* more comfortable I cut a hinged section from the plywood floor of a defunct rubber dinghy. This fitted between the fore-deck and thwart (seat). One of my lidded plastic buckets I replaced with a bright red, oblong, double-skinned picnic box. I hoped the insulated container would relegate melted Mars bars to sticky memories. The red box, together with the centre-board and my new folding section, formed a relatively flat sleeping area.

An indispensable item worth almost its weight in gold was half a battered polystyrene surfboard. I hoped not to need the flotation properties of my ultra-light, waterproof thermal-cushion / life buoy. Before it was added to the inventory I experienced unpleasant hours sitting on the dinghy's floor causing a low point where even the merest trickle of water was sufficient to soak my jeans.

Blue Bosun

The two jib system — dispensing with the gaff and boom for safety's sake, I used again. Another jib of similar size to the original was required — to use as a mainsail. Towards the end of the previous trip I was without a second sail and paid a high price. After being unsuccessful in my quest to obtain a twin sail, having visited several dealers in second-hand nautical bits, I eventually purchased a specimen that had been parted from a Bosun dinghy. It was blue, in fair condition but was three feet too long. I cut the wire that formed one of the sides towards the top of the sail and secured it round a cringle. (A cringle is an eye at the edge of a sail. I do not mean the painted eyes, often of South Sea's origin — talismans to see the sailor safely home. Here I refer to the eye formed from a thimble or grommet. A thimble is like a cringle with no hole in it, except in nautical terms when it is a grommet. A grommet is a cringle, and there you have it.) After trimming away the excess material and folding and taping the cut edge I had produced something unique — a veritable Vivienne Westwood.

From the ground-sheet of a torn two man tent that had belonged to my ten year old Edward, I fashioned a rudimentary detachable shelter. After two wet summers I thought a cover would be a useful addition. The opening end was fastened to the mast and the sides were fixed under the gunwales with loops on to small round-headed screws. Large knots in the heavy blue material held the stern corners in place. Not exactly chic — another touch of the Viviennes, and clashing somewhat with the Blue Bosun. The aft end of this lash-up was raised by a halyard to provide a limited crouching area. The smallness of the enclosure was of no consequence for I intended doing very little crouching. Epic was ready.

Unfavourable Winds

(On to Penryn)

After a pleasant hour ashore at the Smugglers', as dusk was deepening, I rejoined Epic to continue down the Fal. Half a mile on, in darkness, I hitched to another dead tree. This was in an area which would not dry out unlike the previous tree stop. I arranged my bed and had not been in my sleeping-bag more than five minutes when the moon, large and white, rose from behind the treetops and bathed the landscape in silvery half-light — Heaven. Silence was stolen after just five peaceful minutes. On one of two large cargo vessels at anchor a quarter of a mile upriver — just past the King Harry Ferry, a generator erupted into life. Shortly after, my nasal senses were invaded by diesel fumes — Hades. I prepared to exit. Out of my cosy bag I found the night temperature had decreased to an uncomfortable chill. It was about eleven thirty when I finally re-bagged, having rowed a mile or so downstream and round to the right — to the pool below Trelissick House.

My first night afloat on Epic for nearly two years was a very cold affair. The thermal property of my sleeping bag diminished as it soaked up the dew. By the time I listened to the shipping forecast — 5:55, the lower part of the bag and my feet were sopping. The northerly wind would decrease a little but back to the north east — which meant my planned excursions up the Restronguet, Mylor and Penryn creeks were in jeopardy. There was no hint of wind as I breakfasted on Old Jamaica and water. (Old Jamaica was not the yo-ho-ho hard stuff — it was chocolate.) By 6:35 a slight breeze enabled me to boom out the Bosun and head towards Restronguet. It was a gentle sail with the low sun over the stern. The odd fish rose and there was a little cheeping from small birds on the shore and in nearby trees. Further off, spasmodic accompaniment was given by distant raucous rooks.

The warmth of the sun soon eliminated the wrinkled puffiness of my feet which I rested on the transom. The sea was almost flat and Epic moved well in the near calm, passing tree covered mini cliffs to starboard. Just past Feock a seal popped up his head and then popped it back — just a cursory glance, nothing above sea-level to interest him. His taste was savoury — the *visuals* he left for me.

TRELISSICK

'—having rowed a mile or so round to the right—to the pool below Trelissick House.'

A little after 7:00 I beached Epic on the gently shelving, stony Loe Beach. There I painted a group of water-side buildings. It was an unusually early start for me and most rewarding—the low sun angle provided sunlight and shadow. I had to hurry, for the draining tide left the dinghy high and dry and I did not wish to drag the thin, newly painted plywood very far over the stones. The forecast wind wafted away the stillness. My tonal composition was hastily concluded and I pushed off. The breeze hastened me on to Restronguet Point where I came out from the lee. During my hurried withdrawal from the scene I inadvertently left my painting on the fore-deck and was lucky to retrieve it before it was whisked into the briney.

Oars replaced sail and with the pace of the outgoing tide increasing I edged my way energetically but slowly upriver—heading straight into the wind. A few hundred yards past the Pandora Inn, left to port, I fed the painter through the handle of a mooring buoy—it was in fact an old, square, white plastic, gallon bottle encrusted with barnacles. Even though I hugged the left bank there was no way on that tide I could reach Devoran—a mile and a half away at the head of the creek. My sleeping bag that had been on the fore-deck in the sun was still soaking wet so I hoisted it up the mast. I took the opportunity to rig a cord for my new sun-hat. It was of white cotton—the type that cricket players tend to wear these days. It was not so *Jack Tar* as my previous hat—a strong canvas, oatmeal number that had been claimed by Neptune on my last trip. I hoped to become, and remain, attached to the replacement. Waiting for the rising tide, before trying again to ride up Restronguet Creek, I lay down in the boat for a while—to warm up out of the wind. Rest rendered me restless. With time on my hands I decided to pop down to the Pandora for a pint. After lowering my sleeping bag I cast off from the bottle and arrived post-haste at Pandora's pontoon.

Low water was at 1:30 but the falling tide caused me to leave two hours earlier. In no time Epic was back down the creek tied to a large round red buoy—in the shelter of Restronguet Point. A pair of serene swans paid me a visit—at least they looked serene as they sailed over to me. Their combined necks' span was greater than the dinghy's beam. With a probing swan port and starboard my opinion of them, at swan eye-level, was low. It was not a social visit and I was happy, after they had sampled the texture of my clothing, to see them huff off. They were an old couple with scraggy necks—discoloured through dipping. One had a torn upper bill—a piece, a child's small finger size, stuck out in a most uncomfortable looking manner. Poor swan.

To reduce windage I lowered the Bosun, then set off again up the creek. The bare pole would offer a little less resistance without the sail wrapped round it. The wind was even stronger, and I was an hour early, for the tide was still going out — thank you BST. When the water where I had been rowing became an extension of a red/brown, hard mud spit that divided two shallow channels just past the point, all options had been taken from me. Lying down out of the wind, again, I listened to Radio Four. I became aware of two men in a boat, as small as mine, coming slowly down-river. They were endeavouring to head upstream, I assumed — towards the many larger boats that lay on the river bed. They pulled into the shore before being washed out into Carrick Roads. I last saw the ensemble, notably the upturned dinghy, *walking* across the mud and disappearing into the bushes. A spit or so away a man was digging in the mud for worms, I suppose. Tiring of watching the rag or lug prospector I returned to the Afternoon Theatre. Presented through my earphones was the story of a trapped traveller. We had nothing else in common — he was on a train, and not to blame.

Had I waited for the incoming tide to gain momentum I would still have been unable to row into the wind which was gusting strongly. When Epic finally floated I quickly retreated — rounding the point and rushing into and down Carrick Roads to the harbour at Mylor Churchtown — two miles away. With Epic alongside a heavy wooden pontoon in a sheltered corner, I asked at the office if it could remain for half an hour. The northeaster had ruled out a visit up the creek to Mylor Bridge. I sat at an outside table at the Lemon Arms and lunched on coffee and a toasted cheese sandwich. At the time, the chances of not heading up a third creek — to Penryn, was on the cards. The sea condition was too rough to allow myself to be blown past Pendennis Point into Falmouth Bay. It was with uncertainty that I set off for Falmouth Harbour. With just the Bosun set, Epic hurtled for two and a half miles against the tide down to Trefusis Point — opposite Falmouth Docks. To that point I had been sheltered on flattish water and to some extent that was true till I tacked to Flushing. I was about to earn my cheese sandwich.

The channel leading up to Penryn, two miles away, was to the north-west — the direction from which the strong wind still blew. Flushing, like Looe from where I was flushed unwillingly on the last trip, had all the makings of another Waterloo. The waterway was cluttered with boats on moorings — many were large cruising yachts. If progress was to be made I had to tackle the fleet.

After manufacturing the tent/cover I produced *Son of Bosun*. Made from a hole-less portion of tent, it was four feet long and fairly flimsy. It was designed for light airs but I hoped it would be *boy* enough to help Epic head a little more to windward. I felt the wind was too strong to risk using the orange Mirror jib. All seemed to go well at first as I threaded Epic back and forth between the boats. I seemed to be pointing well but made leeway and had to slacken off at times to pass behind vessels and moorings. Half an hour of frustrating tacking — familiarizing myself with certain craft, particularly one with a long bowsprit — just lower than my mast-height, gained me no more than a couple of hundred yards. My performance then became agonizingly abject. Shortly after disentangling my starboard shroud from the familiar bowsprit the little sail blew out and an embarrassed Mirror operative flying a shredded, blue, four foot *burgee,* headed reflectively to the quieter north shore.

With the Bosun down and Son of ready for the first rubbish bin I commenced rowing. It was tough going, even with the in-going tide to help, till I eventually crept past Flushing. Shelter was reached as the creek turned a little more westerly. In a quiet backwater I stepped onto a shingle beach to stretch my legs. Apart from my brief pit stops I had been on board for twenty-four hours. The sky was blue and the wind appeared to be dropping. In good cheer I rowed up to Penryn. While I was floundering around close to the roadside wharfs, the resident of the Humber Keel, Harlequin, invited me to tie up alongside. The Keel is an oddly named class of boat — being flat bottomed and having no keel. The Harlequin is the dwelling of Simon — a singer and musician with a theatre group. His floating home contains a cavernous hold converted to living space. With solid fuel stove, piano and spiral staircase, he still has room to swing several cougars.

After phoning home from the Kings Arms — over the road and up the hill a few paces, I stayed for supper and a pint. I had no wish to remain till closing time — my fix was the uncharted new day ahead. Intoxicated by thoughts of heading seaward again I rejoined Epic and rowed to a pool a few hundred yards round the corner from the road bridge. With surprising ease I rigged the tent and was soon lulled to sleep in a small blue world.

FLUSHING, FROM PENRYN

'Flushing, like Looe from where I was flushed unwillingly on the last trip —'

25

Fish and Creeks
(Penryn to Helford)

Epic grounded around midnight and refloated about 4:00. I cannot be exact for I slept soundly. The soft mud gently claimed and cradled Epic and in due course released her to swing against the incoming tide. At five-to-six I listened to the force three to four forecast. A wind blowing down-channel was expected — just right.

It had been another dewy night and my canopy was dripping with an incomprehensible amount of water. The same was true of the varnished boat interior — it was as if it had rained inside the tent during the night. From ashore it would have appeared that I was boat-proud in the extreme as I sponged all surfaces and hoisted aloft the dripping *rain machine* and sleeping bag.

Chores completed, I took breakfast — two bananas and water. It sounds pretty dull fare but did not seem so at the time. The most mundane food items became manna. I remember finding quite a large crisp on board — it had somehow escaped and miraculously settled in a sheltered corner. Opening a bag of crisps when sailing or rowing in windy weather is not always foolproof — and I should know. Finding the salt and vinegar flavoured delicacy later and allowing it to melt on my tongue was almost sacramental.

Before utilizing the fair wind I decided to produce a painting of the boat-sheds — towards the head of the river. By 7:00, with moist items up the mast — catching the sun, I was rowing round to Penryn. To my right, moored bow to bank, were a couple of dozen boats. Some occupied house boats, some laid up boats and some laid to rest — terminal cases with extreme submarine tendencies. In close proximity to the boats I tied to a mooring and began a painting featuring a large boat-shed with shady recesses. Sunlight on boats in front of the dark open-ended building was an important element. The cloud cover increased to seventy five percent as I worked. (You didn't think I was on holiday.) During a spell, waiting for the sun, I perceived my perusal by a river-dweller. He may have wondered from where I got my blue sky but could see that my invasion of his *garden* was harmless. What I was to take away would still remain, give or take a few clouds.

At 9:30 I rowed to the top corner of Penryn Harbour. Cloud cover was forty percent and decreasing—typical. Life on board Epic was serene. I drifted down-river past the Harlequin and with a following wind went Bosuning to Flushing. While Epic was tied close to the steps at the Fisherman's Jetty I climbed up and walked across to the Quay Restaurant. Sitting outside, outnumbered by the staff of two, I enjoyed a coffee in the sunshine—the little white clouds had become few in number. I was sheltered from the gentle though slightly increasing breeze. The pleasant young ladies assured me Epic would not be in the way while I went to restock my red picnic box with crisps, chocolate and Mars bars. Such an understanding attitude I found most common. (The unfortunate encounter at St Germans during my last trip was very rare—I was turned away. I have since been contacted by the Quay Yacht Club. Virtually all the members were displeased with their non-representative. Visitors are welcome and they now have a sign to prove it.)

Opulent Flushing looked well cared for—even a gigantic redundant oil-rig moored in Carrick Roads seemed to know its place. The tower, which I thought possessed great out of context sculptural power, lurked discreetly round the headland.

While crossing to Falmouth I scribbled in my logbook/diary, 'Stopped while rowing (11:51) over to Fal. to say I'm the luckiest person alive'. Had I not stopped to jot, that moment of utter contentment would have been forgotten—filtered from my mind by other passages that were not so enjoyable. My happiness was as great then, full with optimistic eagerness at the prospect of leaving Carrick Roads, as it was two years before when I had escaped into Carrick Roads from the open sea.

Keeping close in to the Falmouth foreshore I viewed at leisure the various slip-ways and quays—both private and public. Such structures, grandly restored or derelict, formed an incredible hotchpotch that exuded a *sailory* excitement. I would not go so far as to say, *I conjured from empty air, sounds and smells of the age of sail. The tang of tar and oakum, cracking canvas and straining spars.* (Who said that?) It will help set the scene though if you imagine the *bounding main* music that boisterously accompanied old pirate film sagas.

A real taste of bygone working sail boats is still presented off Falmouth. The back windows of shops that front the main street provide a panoramic view of the vintage racers. I cannot be the only weekend shopper who has found his mission impossible — tempted from purchasing by sails seen through windows — drawn to the waterfront by old gaffers jousting about — awed by the straight stemmed, long bow-sprit sporting craft, carrying multitudes of heavy canvas triangles as they race in thundering flocks through crowded moorings.

After reaching the end of the town's waterfront I rowed a hundred yards or so off-shore and hitched to a mooring off Custom House Quay. Ahead in the docks were several large ocean-going ships, being or having been refitted. They were unladen, elevated on vast slabs of tan antifouled hull. When returned to commerce their destinations would always be more distant but unlikely to be more beautiful than my next area of investigation just round the corner — the Helford River.

The wind was quite fresh away from the shelter of the buildings, reminding me to don my life jacket as I prepared for the open sea. The jacket, comprising front and collar only, is secured round the waist by tapes. Do not imagine me as Michelin man — I wear it virtually deflated and it is not at all cumbersome. The nifty little number can be worn under a jumper and be quickly inflated by mouth if the need arises. The Bosun I hoisted and furled round the mast — ready for rapid deployment. After tidying away all loose gear — stowing it in the fore-deck mini-compartments and beneath my new folding fore-deck extension, I was ready to sail to the creeks of intrigue — as designated by Daphne. Within a few hours the wood-fringed waterways would begin to fill with a new tide — my gratis ride to upper reaches.

I first had to negotiate the dock area. Oar-power was required for I was hemmed in by a five hundred yard barrier of wharf-bays. The structure was composed of ranks of giant legs formed from huge timbers. The shady labyrinths seemed an ideal setting for mysterious operations — space to secrete many midget Bond subs. At least ninety percent of my effort was expended in counteracting the wind and the out-going stream — they combined to make me earn my freedom. Though not a herculean task, my progress past the pillars was pitifully slow.

FALMOUTH

'Keeping close in to the Falmouth foreshore I viewed at leisure the various slip-ways and quays —'

The reward was more than fair compensation when escape from the docks was eventually achieved. With the oars resting along the gunwales, the Bosun pulled me past the be-castled headland of Pendennis. Soon Epic and I were chuckling across Falmouth Bay.

I lay with my head resting on my hands, elbows on the foredeck, torso on the folding deck modification and legs on the red picnic box. The prone position presented less resistance to the offshore beam wind and provided me with a great deal of fun as I steered with my feet and held the brim of my hat up against the lower edge of the sail in order to see. With my hands free I was able to make notes and use my compass and Ordnance Survey map to determine direction. Although only four miles distant the Helford River mouth was not apparent as I looked obliquely along the coastline. Finding my way was not at all difficult, but I was in play mode and indulged in a little *Captain Cookery*. With my limited equipment I practised navigation. Not surprisingly I received a few refreshing face-fulls of spray as the flat hull slapped the little waves — my eye-level was little more than one foot above sea level. The low vantage point did nothing to dampen my high sea spirits.

Before the playful spray ceased being a novelty, the breeze lessened and my arrival off the Helford River was completed with one further ado — a slight contact with a slightly underwater August Rock. A quarter mile off Mawnan, between Rosemullion Head and the River, that rock is the only blemish on the pale blue area of Falmouth Bay on OS 204 — some navigator. Such a brush in a dinghy as light as Epic is not too serious in fair conditions. Similar contact in a heavier boat could mean some structural rearrangement — not too serious for the rock.

In the dying wind I enjoyed a pleasant sail to a point where the river narrows to three hundred yards. The fitful breeze caused an enjoyable delay — I had no wish to chase the yachts that motored past. Tacking allowed me to view in detail both shores as the tide moved Epic slowly onwards. Discreet, small scale architectural structures on the southern side of the river entrance added sympathetic additions to the wooded hillsides and rocky foreshore. A circular fortification near the mouth and an octagonal mini look-out construction were ideal elements to form the bases for paintings. A touch of man's geometry, particularly when rustically aged, can add an interesting focal point to nature's pretty competent arrangements.

At the narrow point just before Helford Passage on the right and Helford Village to the left, I downed sail and commenced a spell of lazy rowing. All was quiet. With inns both sides of the river I resisted the temptation to visit either — having succumbed to the soothing tranquillity. At 5:00 I found my idyll interrupted in the nicest possible way. Off Frenchman's Creek, three miles into the river, a hissing tide-race sound caused me to look round and wonder at the disturbed surface area. Totalling two or three hundred square yards the broken water contained rushing swirling arcs. Had I been able to see beneath the reflective surface, the unidentified marine objects would have become identified M O's — fish. The shoal, I imagine, was feeding on tiny aquatic foodstuff and in turn became supper for bigger hunters.

Soon I left Groyne Point to my right, opting not to head towards Constantine — favouring the Gweek and not the Roman Creek. Up-river a few hundred yards a group of young people were enjoying a barbecue. They had travelled to the secluded spot in dinghies which were tied alongside Tremayne Quay. I increased my row rate a little and rippled on upstream to leave them in peace. The quay was built for a visit by Queen Victoria — but she did not make it. It was pleasing to see that a century and a half later the work had not been wasted. (You may have wondered at the lack of architectural and historical information in this discourse. Had I mentioned all the sites, from old large stones to defunct mine workings, and the famous and infamous who trod, or like Queen Vic. nearly trod, I would have risked lapsing into over seriousness.)

Gweek is at the head of the river, six miles in from the sea. As the in-going tide slackened I found the last two miles, into a fresh breeze, a hard slog. Until then I had been sheltered from the wind in a tree-lined section. At a fork in the river I turned right, leaving behind the entrance to a sheltered, mysterious looking creek that led to Trelowarren Mill — half a mile away. My instinct for exploration was overruled by my desire for food. I required an inn, which I was sure to find at Gweek. At 7:45 I tied little Epic alongside a varied collection of larger craft. There were rugged house-boat types that could have started life as fishing vessels, and serious sailing boats undergoing extensive refits for serious cruising.

For a while I sat outside The Black Swan listening to live brass band music, wondering from whence it came. Why was I the only outdoor patron I also wondered? It came to me as my hot vegetarian curry arrived. It was rather chilly (not the curry). My earlier exertions had made me oblivious to the falling temperature. I hurried my curry and withdrew to sup a pint in congenial warmth. Alas I could not dally, for as my glass was emptying so too was the river. The boats and banks were becoming silhouettes and the lower sky was reflecting orange onto the water. As I made my way back to Epic the band blew up again. Gweek Silver Band (I learned their name, and the colour of their instruments later) were practising in a tiny building — just down from the pub. Though I saw no alterative venue I had not even considered the possibility of the music coming from so small a place — it must have been jammed full of metal and musicians. With the accompaniment of distant silver *sardine* band music I boarded Epic and helped by wind and tide, rowed into the chill dusk.

After several minutes, from the deepening darkness there came a finale from nature's repertoire — a sound like the barking moo of an unhappy cow. Realizing my proximity — I had just passed Gweek's famous seal sanctuary, I thought it must be the call from a contented inmate, unable to sound melodious even when given free fish. Towards the end of my immensely enjoyable day, I was also content as I made my way silently into the night.

I decided to sleep in Frenchman's Creek. It was almost dark as I neared the junction where a great number of the small fish were rising. At several splashes per second I assumed the shoal, of previous acquaintance, was midnight-supping on flies — yummy. Leaving the feasting fish behind I entered the narrowing stretch of water. I must admit to finding the creek eerie. Between the dark crowding banks, limbs from dead tree obstructions faintly fingered the fading sky. With Epic hitched for a third time to a deceased deciduous I lay down in my sleeping bag — under the tent which I had no desire to rig. An hour or so later the Mirror grounded at an extremely uncomfortable angle. The dead tree had caused a build up of creek-bed round its submerged boughs and on that slope I suffered. The water exited rapidly and I became a reclining statue, unable to move lest I roll over the three inches of protective freeboard into the ooze — which I imagined to be soft and bottomless. I would have to step into the mud at some point but forced myself to endure a fitful sleep.

FRENCHMAN'S CREEK

'— a lone swan interrupted the tranquillity — disturbing the glassy surface upstream —'

At 5:00, after gingerly extricating myself from the wet bag and tent, I found myself at a low ebb. The only way was up—and so it was. I slipped my icy socked feet into my new fluffy lined wellies and avoiding squelchy areas stepped onto a surprisingly firmish surface. To counteract the cold I wandered along the wooded, twilit waterside for a while, reminding my legs of their purpose. The early half-light of a new day revealed those large rounded root-tops, upholstered with spongy moss, where hobbits or other nether-world creatures might be encountered. On returning I glimpsed Epic through the trees as the mist-shrouded river crept towards the tiny craft. Like a Tolkien illustration she was held in a sinister entanglement of weed-festooned branches. The exercise lifted me to the warmer side of freezing. Under a clear sky that coldly held a half full moon I returned as the incoming tide lapped the listing Epic. By the time my wellies were swilled and glistening on the wet stern seat I was afloat. It was 5:45. Every item aboard that was not in a polythene bag or on my person was wringing wet as usual. I headed to the mouth of Frenchman's Creek to find the sun.

Anna Hill's early shipping forecast came through the earphones. First with good news, 'North west three . . . ' a wind to take me from the Helford, out round Nare Point and down the coast. Then ' . . . backing south west, four to five . . . ' a wind to deny an approach to Coverack. Anna may be wrong, I hoped—after all I was on the up.

At 6:15 a lone swan interrupted the tranquillity—disturbing the glassy surface upstream as it surged towards the sound of a bar of Bournville being broached. I felt I had to reward my energetic visitor and placed a precious square on the gunwale. As if to say 'What no weed' he beaked the offering to the bottom.

A little later I was floating around the creek mouth, warming myself in the early sunshine. I had hoisted the damp bag—it was becoming a custom, like raising the flag. The fish had come in again on the tide and I found myself in the centre of a splashing, flapping circus. Shortly after, a flock of small gulls with black heads joined the fray. They also went crazy. There are times when you have to escape from the hurly-burly. Leaving nature to it I headed back up the creek to explore its upper reaches. With my back resting on the painting stool and feet raised to the sun I made my way lazily back past the submerging mooring tree. I kept to the sunny side where my *pennant* bag cast a shadow, contouring the trees just above the darker water-line area. Less than a mile away the creek petered out in a confusion of fallen trees. I turned Epic round and headed out of the *novel* creek, singing, 'I'm on the road to Mand-er-lay-ay-ay, where the flying-fishes play, da, da di da . . . ' *Rebecca Visits Frenchman's Creek.*

After an enjoyable wind-assisted ride down to the pontoon at Helford Point I wandered round the headland to the picturesque Helford Village. Dwellings are situated on the protected slopes of an inlet. Featured at waterside is the Shipwrights Arms — the thatched inn that I nobly left in my wake the previous evening. I knew of the hidden pub but the Helford River held competing enchantments on that balmy night. Perhaps some pleasures are best left for a rainy day — oh blessed British climate. After walking through the village — right up to the top of the hill and right down again, I made a bee-line for Rose Cottage tea garden. Checking my watch for the nearness of lunch-time I found it to be about four hours away. Enquiring into opening times I was fortunate to make the acquaintance of Kit, the lady of the garden. She opened half an hour early and invited me to take a seat in her sunny retreat. Sufficient satisfaction should have been provided by my near complete bar of cold chocolate taken earlier but I exercised the necessary lack of will-power. My request, ''Possibly some toast?'' started the slide. A mention of bacon tipped the balance. Then I was sunk, coup de grâced by the great outdoor fried bacon aroma that wafted from the kitchen. Eggs, beans, buttered toast and marmalade, a large pot of tea and a glass of fresh orange followed, putting me in sublime cheer. I left the small terraced garden — Eden by another name, knowing it would not be in the spirit of this tale to commute to Helford for breakfast each morning.

In a prominent elevated position — on the point at Helford Point, rests an old, chunky wooden seat. There I sat for a few contemplative minutes before making my way back to Epic. Looking down-river and out to sea I knew my destiny lay to the right, but where and in what form I knew not. *Cue the sea saga music.* The excitement was tempered by frustration. To my left, clouds were taking away the blue and those low down were decidedly dark. It seemed Anna might be right.

Beaten Back

(Helford to Porthoustock)

By 11:00 there was full cloud and the wind was getting up—blowing down-river. I attached both sails but left them furled while I rowed out against the wind that had been pressing Epic onto the pontoon. Soon the Bosun was taking me out of the Helford River. Fifteen minutes later it was raining. A sharp right-hander out of the estuary and you are in Gillan Harbour. This natural inlet at the mouth of a mile long creek has a lesser St Anthony on the north shore and a lesser Flushing on the south. A stranger blundering into this peaceful backwater might wonder at the rearrangement and shrinking of Carrick Roads. It was quite pleasant pottering around the sheltered confines in the light greyness. A group of hardy youngsters, quite beyond the call of duty, were swimming. Their bravery set me a-girding—I decided to use the last of the outgoing tide and the offshore west wind, which was reaching its useful maximum for me, to head the three miles to Porthallow for a rain-check. I rounded a lesser Nare Head—the proper big one is to the east of Carrick Roads, and headed south.

Buoyant, only in the physical sense, I completed the short and uneventful passage. My upward well-being trend was levelled off by the continuing weather low. The offshore wind made beaching at Porthallow a simple and dry operation. With the tide almost out and Epic tethered to a heavy stone on the grey shingle I could remain uncooped for an hour or so. Free-ranging up the beach I passed a row of fishing boats, winched above the high-tide line, and chanced upon the Five Pilchards pub. It was just after 2:30. I stood outside and read, 'Closed 2:30—7:00'. *If chalk-boards had minds of their own, that one I am sure would have added 'so there'*. A little way up the hill I entered a secluded tea garden—it was just a phase I was going through. Soon I was genteelly quenching with tea and enjoying a large piece of home-made cake. Again I was the sole customer—as if I were on a crusade not to allow waterside caterers to be customerless. As I weighed the chances of the wind dropping with the lady of the cake—a horticulturist of obvious skill, a potted plant was blown from a nearby wall and, omen-like, the pot smashed. Had it hit me on the head, I may have taken heed. Back down on the beach I asked the most senior-looking fisherman if he thought I would be safe going on the two miles to Porthoustock. I set off with an affirmative, qualified with a suggestion that I keep well inshore.

HELFORD

'Soon the Bosun was taking me out of the Helford River.'

I made swift progress till Porthoustock was abeam. Another grey shingle beach, this time guarded by a forty foot high, rectangular concrete silo — built for crushed stone loading. It was defunct and its sombre presence suggested a stark fortification. Ahead was Manacle Point, ending with a row of four or five mini mountains reaching seaward. The tide was turning against me but there was more than enough wind so I decided to carry on. Instead of rounding the ten to fifteen feet high outcrops I aimed for the gap between obstruction numbers three and four — in from the sea. I lost the wind in the narrow channel at the moment the swell lowered Epic against a not sufficiently submerged rock. I swiftly hauled out the centre-board and soon had the chaos in full swing. The oars made contact with both sides of the channel. The laces that held the oars to the rowlocks and the rowlocks to the gunwhale were quite a hindrance. I tried to push off with one oar and then paddle, indian-style, with a swinging galvanized rowlock clanging against rock and hull. Epic lost some of her new white gunwhale paint as she scraped down the barnacled rock surfaces and was lucky not to tip on projecting ledges. The whole voyage was a learning process. Short cuts can be dangerous and can waste a lot of time, and that's on a good day.

Once in the clear I tacked down the coast, close inshore, well inside the Manacles — a group of sinister rocks that lie one mile out to sea. The threatening cluster, mostly hidden at high tide, has claimed numerous vessels. Many masters of trading sailing ships, on bad days in the past, paid the ultimate price for corner cutting.

Black clouds were gathering. Progress was slow — I was pushing against the tide. When three miles on from Porthallow — having travelled considerably further through the water, I sighted Coverack between Lowland Point and Great Wrea — another group of rocks. Three times I tried to make it past that final barrier before Coverack. The two sails provided plenty of power. Back in Carrick Roads I had been so timid with Son of Bosun. I had since learnt how far to push Epic, or so I thought. My offshore tacks had to be terminated each time when a few hundred yards out — the sea condition being too much to cope with. The tide was more rapid at the Point — against me, and my inshore tacks ended inside the Great Wrea. It was just as well, for had I got round I feel the wind that had backed south west would have deposited Epic on the lee shore. Safety, in the stretch of water protected by the high land round Coverack, lay tantalizingly just a mile away.

I did something rather foolish on my last tack out. In an attempt to reduce windage I lay down and steered by feet as before. The jib-sheet I locked in the clam-cleat* and the Bosun sheet I squeezed into a flimsy plastic hook fitting and put a turn round the port rowlock for safety. I crashed along at a fair pace grasping the gunwales tightly to stay on board. Both sails bulged tautly under the strain and tipped the dinghy to the point where she used all her precious few inches of freeboard. As Epic was about to put her lee gunwhale under I tried to push the helm down—to turn into the wind and release the pressure on the sails. My foot slipped from the tiller and I fell to the side, restraining myself on the shroud.** I released the jib-sheet as I was joined in the watery starboard side of the boat by my red picnic box and other odds and ends. Nothing went overboard. Broadside to the wind, I spent a frantic few seconds releasing the *safely* set Bosun sheet. Instantly I found myself in a relatively peaceful, vertical, safe though damp situation, drifting north-eastwards. There was plenty of time to reflect and take stock before the odd Manacle could intervene. I headed back down the coast—keeping well inshore of course. It is so easy to become careless and disregard signs of danger. Such disconcerting occurrences should reinforce respect and make one less vulnerable.

For the first time since leaving Morwellham Quay at the start of the voyages I had to retreat—discounting the minor incident at Restronguet Creek. On my slow way out to Lowland Point I had passed close by a pier. Alongside was a large cargo boat waiting to take on crushed grey stone from a conveyor running along high gantries. The pier was only half a mile from the Point. A small sandy beach was situated at the west side and there I landed. I jumped off as the hull touched the sand, and with the help of a breaking wave hauled Epic a few yards up the beach. The loading of the cargo boat had just commenced and I wondered how long it would take to convey ten thousand tons of stone (my estimate). I hoped to leave Epic at the quarry but would need help. While the big boat loading commenced I removed the sails and unloaded most of Epic's gear—stacking it at the top of the beach. Though the waves at the time were little flippers—no more than a foot high, I had to keep rushing to Epic's aid as she turned broadside and pounded on the beach, taking fountains of sandy water up the centre case.

* Spring loaded, toothed cams that tighten when under pressure. A sheet can be released with a reverse pull and lifting.
** One of the three wires that hold the mast up. The front one is the fore-stay.

With my charge tethered to a long painter I passed a depressing hour fending off. I landed at 7:00 — two hours before high tide. I munched Old Jamaica and Bournville in the drizzle as I watched the surprisingly rapid loading of the chippings. The stern sank low into the water then the bow — to level the boat. In great haste mooring lines were slipped and the vessel reversed out to sea. At that moment, *Spock beamed up the loading overseers* — they vanished from the pier. Perhaps the men thought I was waiting for someone in particular. Because of their disappearance I felt no embarrassment — standing alone tending several gallons of sandy salt-water in the bottom of my Mirror dinghy.

Moving Epic to a safe position on my own — up the steep slope at the back of the beach away from the threat of rough seas, would have been rather precarious. Besides, I did not wish to leave the dinghy, as if *beamed down* — it may have been beach-combed before I could inform the quarrymen of my ongoing intentions. I bailed out, reset the Bosun, reloaded, pushed off and shot back to Porthoustock. There I beached Epic behind the giant silo on a patch of soft grey sand. When I was sure the tide had turned I left Epic and phoned home — to ask the reliant Robin if he would collect me.

A handful of fishing-boats around twenty feet long had been winched above the tide-line — as was the custom. A little way up the beach where the grey pebbles were large, two fishermen were working on a boat. They were sure it would be in order to leave the dinghy close by, awaiting fair weather. I left Epic on the sand and walked over to the 3 Tuns at St Keverne — where I had arranged to meet my chauffeur.

The oddly named pub was no more than a mile and a half from Porthoustock. As the first half mile required gaining considerable altitude my need for a refreshing pint had moved on from 'I don't mind if I do' status, to, 'Perhaps if I lay under the tap . . . ' Later, having upturned Epic on the big stones, Robin and I loaded the car with mast, oars and the remaining damp, sandy clutter.

Starting at Frenchman's Creek, my long and eventful day had been punctuated with disappointment and pantomime. Despite being battered, bruised and beaten back, I was surprisingly content when returned to Mevagissey a little ahead of pumpkin time. Oh yes I was.

PORTHOUSTOCK

'I left behind a relaxed holiday scene.'

41

Fire-Light Landing

(Porthoustock to The Lizard)

I waited for fair weather. Week followed week. Favourable conditions were required for rounding the Lizard. I waited. I waited four full weeks. After hearing the early shipping forecast on Thursday 5th August I hoped my waiting was over. Walking down the garden later that morning, to collect the oars from the studio, I found the wind still quite strong. I pondered as I picked and ate a handful of dark red, wild strawberries. The few clouds, although not hanging about, were high and white. The sun felt hot — a taste of real summer. Epic called.

While eating a bacon sandwich, purchased from a man in a van in a lay-by en route to Porthoustock, I jotted, ' . . . west north-west four to five, occasionally six, decreasing three. Bacon sandwich good, wind direction good, decreasing three — delicious.' Edward, Robin and I continued on our way. A week or so earlier, Julia and I had visited Epic — safe and upside-down on the big stones. It was gratifying to find her still there, unmolested. Thank you Porthoustock.

Hardly helped by a very light offshore breeze, the boys set off from the grey shingle for a sample sail. For half an hour, mostly rowing, they cruised the bay while I sat nervously in the car. I was not too worried at leaving my borrowed distress flare behind, or where I would spend the night. I suppose my long absence from the water had allowed a modicum of pessimism to manifest itself.

Sometime after 4:00 I stepped into Epic, rowed out a little way and set both sails. The car was driven away and I waved goodbye to the boys. I left behind a relaxed holiday scene. Two small dinghies provided fun afloat and a dozen or so people, mostly children, were doing their own things at the water-line. As I was leaving the bay my concentration was knocked out of neutral — I missed by a foot, a tip of rock that just broke the surface. It was a not too distant, young relation of Manacle Point. With many a salutary glance over my shoulder I passed the headland for a second time — giving it a respectable berth.

Alone again. No worries for a while. The simple task, or pleasure, of cruising from A to B. Perhaps not knowing where B is till it becomes A — if you see what I mean. I passed close to the quarry pier then déjà vu'd along to Lowland Point — the previous point of return. I was soon laying on my back, feet steering fast through crab-pot marker flags to B — Coverack.

Off Coverack, I noted shorthandedly, 'WNW 4 5 DC3 M F G' – almost identical to the bacon sandwich forecast, but thankfully without the 'OC 6' – occasionally six. M F G = mainly fair, good – referring to visibility. I liked to think that the 'good', that often ended an area sequence, was Anna or colleague saying 'that's alright then'.

Just past the harbour I tied Epic to the far side of the lifeboat slip. There was just room to ride to a short painter between the slip and rocky shore. The wind held the dinghy away from the old solid wooden structure. It was perfect – I was able to step ashore easily at boat level.

After four weeks delay I was anxious to get on. I stayed just forty five minutes at Coverack. Time enough to inspect the pretty little harbour, full with water and boats strung tidily in lines – bow to stern. Harbours look so much better when the tide is in. There were twenty or so smaller craft by the slip-way at the harbour edge. The scene was one of total tranquillity. People carried out their inactivity in the sunshine – mostly sheltered from the breeze by the harbour wall. I did not dally. I refuelled on apple pie and cream, a large mug of coffee and a half pint of Newquay Steam at the Paris Hotel – close to the harbour. 'Yes, just a half' – I noted in my log.

The next leg of the voyage did not turn out as I had expected – still a learning process. High tide was around 7:45 and I left about an hour earlier. I thought there would be little tidal movement, and eventually when the English Channel did start to empty into the Atlantic I would be taken towards Cadgwith – five or six miles away. There was quite a swell off Chynhalls Point – just half a mile on. The low roar as the surges rose and drained from the rocks seemed out of place considering the sheltered aspect. I steered with the wind on my left cheek. Looking back I saw the Dodman – still faintly visible though twenty miles away. A potent odour of cow manure came to me for a few seconds and I was pleased to be no nearer the source. To we land persons, what we think is the smell of the sea is the smell of the land to those who venture far offshore. It is, cows permitting, the seashore/seaweed smell. Enough of manure. In another mile, after taking a sharp right round Black Head I lost site of the Dodman. Between the headland and off-lying rocks I first sighted The Lizard. The sun shone from behind pinnacles that spiked from the sea. Motionless, elongated black sea-birds austerely decorated the *Gothic* rocks. That point also marked the fiftieth parallel. Just three miles of the British mainland protrudes into the forties (degrees latitude, north) – the end of the Lizard Peninsular.

At 7:00 pm I set a course for – aimed at, Cadgwith, which I hoped to enjoy for longer than my flying visit to Coverack. I imagined the passage would be swift, for Epic cut through the water at a fair speed. As it became darker I had difficulty gauging my progress. I was heading into the setting sun and the land was in silhouette. Although time was slipping by I did not think anything was amiss, till a buoy forming a wake appeared to overtake me. I expected a fair tide but found my speed through the water was insufficient to compete with a stationary buoy. The sea was taking me back to Coverack. I was about half a mile offshore when I hurriedly downed sail and rowed in close to the cliffs to escape the full force of the tide.

'8:15, sighted the Lizard again' – through the rocks at Black Head and re-crossed, again, the fiftieth parallel. Keeping as tight in to the hostile coastline as I dared, I rowed between rocks and mini islands the three miles to Kennack Sands – due west in the corner of the bay. With a fresh cold wind on my back the row seemed to take a long time. In fact it was one hour – one very long hour. When I approached the beach it was nearly dark with a touch of pink in the sky. I was guided by a fire on the beach. Until virtually upon it I did not notice a reef blocking my way. The ragged hazard protruded just a foot or two above the surface and I was lucky to notice it against the fire-light. Having rowed round the reef I was about to beach when a man out walking with his family shouted to me to head in a few yards to my right. He waved me over to an area free from rocks and with his shoes and socks off entered the sea. The Samaritan in helping Epic in on a little wave was rewarded with wet trousers. I had been in no danger. He just wanted to help – to save Epic from possible damage.

After bailing out the few gallons of sea that entered over the stern I set off for the pub – a few hundred yards away up a steep hill. The man who helped me land said I would find a phone there – most convenient. The tide was receding and would return to meet Epic after the early forecast – which was also very convenient. On leaving the Kennack Sands Hotel an hour or so later I was greeted by a huge, round orange moon as it rose over the hill. Revealed in silhouette was the dark reef – the falling tide showed more of the grandly sinister obstruction. A reflected fiery lunar road pointed straight towards Mevagissey – I felt a bit lonely. Behind the beach was an area of rough grass. There beside a little stream I lay down in my bag, enfolded within the mutilated tent.

COVERACK

'— boats strung tidily in lines — bow to stern.'

Despite the late start my hands were already sore and my back ached. At the beginning of each leg I was over-optimistic — expecting to be wafted effortlessly to each new B. I had not regained the rhythm of the voyage — was only at *half* with nature, out of tune with the tidal flow. I slept — topping up with optimism.

Several times during the night I woke, 'V cold night. No gloves.' — I noted. Huge Bondi Beach breakers pounded the shore during the night — I thought. The *twidark* confirmed it — I thought. When there was light enough to assess the difficulty of launching through the giant waves I looked from the beach-head and saw the jaunty little Epic, blunt bow slightly raised, pointing a stumpy mast towards the Lizard. Of huge rollers there were none. A small wave would form periodically and collapse in slow-motion along the length of the beach. That such a timid act of nature could produce such volume was quite extraordinary. In the clear morning sky, when most of the night had lightened away, I saw a prize shooting star. A bright light-line, fast and silent, marked its oblivion.

At 5:30, with head-phones under my woolly hat, I stalked the beach. I had slow marched a sandy half mile, with log book at the ready and pen wedged between frozen fingers, when the Walkman delivered and I doodled — 'Danny Boy, Up She Rises' and 'Men of Harlech'. The rousing tunes were followed by the shipping forecast. The prediction was perfect, ' . . . variable three', after an offshore beam wind that would take me to the Lizard.

By the time I was ready to load the soggy sleeping-bag and tent, the tide was approaching Epic's stern. Close to the port side lay a number of rocks and large pebbles in a mini sand canyon. They had been excavated by the little stream as it meandered across the beach. The rocks were quite angular and up to a foot or so across — it was the hazard I had been saved from the previous night.

A small amount of water came aboard up the centre-board case as I launched. Soon I welcomed the sun — a hill had shielded the beach in the early hours. In no time the ground-sheet / tent and sail bag were hoisted to dry. On an oily calm I rowed towards Enys Head. '7:01, EPIC LEAKS!!' my pen exclaimed, as if Epic's life expectancy was to be measured in minutes. I sponged a pint or so overboard and did likewise a short while later. To my great relief Epic became dry again. After beaching at Kennack Sands, water must have drained into the rear buoyancy / seat compartment and seeped back out when the boat was afloat and horizontal.

Luxuriating in sunny silence I hugged the coast. In less than a mile I chanced upon Carleon Cove. Twin stone buildings, a lonely three storey warehouse and a disused circular structure, tempted me to land — with the view to paint. Rocky outcrops on the scrubby hillsides, shadows cast by the low sun and a dwelling peeping over trees a little way back from the beach, presented me with a fine composition. The plan was to step sprightly onto a boulder and as the slight swell receded push Epic away by foot. I would be ashore with the dinghy bobbing about at the end of a long painter. Perhaps it was a larger than average surge I chose, for as I disembarked it surged on and filled my left wellington. Precariously holding on to Epic I tottered till the next swell arrived then tumbled aboard — defeated.

At 7:50 am, a hundred yards offshore just below the fiftieth parallel, a lone mariner with white legs pinkening in the sunshine, sat rinsing his left sock in fresh water. A pair of jeans with wet left leg dangled from a halyard. They hung aloft with tent and life-jacket, soon to be joined by a wet sock. The *Mirror-man* headed south.

On arrival at Cadgwith, just a mile on, I pulled Epic on to the shingle, wandered a few yards up the beach and sat on a slipway wall. There I ate cheese and chutney sandwiches — prepared at home. My breakfast of tangy cheese and sweet chutney I took at 9:15-ish. The sandwiches had a day to amalgamate into a succulent experience that delighted my eager taste-buds. There was just a handful of people coming and going. A fisherman was working on an engine in one of thirty or so smallish boats on the beach. I fancied a cup of something hot, and as I had to wait an hour for a cafe to open, I wandered round the corner to the Devil's Frying-pan. After a few minutes of leisurely ambling between stone and thatched cottages I looked down into the very large, crater-like hole. A pool at the bottom led to the sea via a cave of story-book intrigue. The Frying Pan was barely simmering. In rough weather the giant cauldron becomes a confined maelstrom — angry seas surge through the cave tunnel to create a hellish scene. I left to have a cup of tea.

The fine shingle beach was quite steep, making it a simple matter to drag Epic back into the sea. At 11:00 I went out of Cadgwith and into the Frying Pan. It was a magical experience. Sunlight shone into the *crater* and enough light was reflected underwater to distinguish the entrance from other caves. The rocky ceiling seemed very low at first but as I got nearer I thought the mast-head might fit through — and so it did. The dark water in the cave rose and fell lazily — no more than a foot or two but enough to make me anxious. There was little room to manipulate the oars and squeeze through to the bright clear water where projections beneath the surface were no longer imagined. The tide would have been too high an hour earlier to allow even Epic's dumpy little mast to scrape into the Frying Pan.

Soon I progressed from the salt-stained and sticky-tape mended Ordnance Survey, Landranger 204 which had helped me from Mevagissey. I entered map 203 — the fourth and most dramatic sheet used since setting out on the Tamar. It featured on the cover a photograph of the rugged cliffs at Land's End with agitated white water beneath. I still held the wish to take Epic round that most westerly point of England. At the time it was still very much a dream. Landranger 203 also depicted The Lizard — the most southerly point of England just two and a half inches, or two miles away.

How different it was then, rowing gently and aided by the tide, than had been the battle to Kennack Sands the previous evening. The deserted coast-line, unmolested by man's hand, held a powerful grandeur. The landscape was a harmonious combination of muted colours. A lightly clouded pale sky was reflected much darker in the blue sea. A little lighter was the turquoise tinge close in below the barnacled ochre of the lower cliffs. A purple-black band above the barnacles was topped by saffron-yellow, salt-sprayed, lichen. The rolling hills were draped in dry yellow green and scarred by stone outcrops of burnt sienna, greys and an occasional flash of newly fractured, glinting granite. (Painters, dust your palette with earthy subtlety. Forsake wincing greens and yellows of excessive acid.)

CADGWITH

'The fine shingle beach was quite steep, making it a simple matter to drag Epic back into the sea.'

I was thinking of seeking advice on suitable tides and times for rounding the Lizard when I sighted, between the mainland and Whale Rock, the lifeboat building and slip at Church Cove. I was perplexed – expecting to see a church on a sandy beach. The Cove I had in mind is on the other side of the Lizard – beyond Mullion. A rash of Gull Rocks around the coast I was aware of, but the outbreak of Church Coves on the Lizard was quite surprising.

As I slipped through the inviting channel by the big black Whale Rock, rascally little rocks broke the surface. So with backward glances, towards where I was going, I headed to Church Cove – half a mile away, for orders. (The rowing position may confuse the reader somewhat as well as the one who bumps into things.) There was a bit of a swell that made me think twice about landing. I dithered a while before heading onto the rough shingle area, below a steep slip that led up to half a dozen stone dwellings. The annoying surge prevented my leaving Epic for more than a few seconds. I was unable to explore or seek life in the peaceful, beyond my desire at the time, village. In consolation I took two photographs. One of *Mary Celeste* Cove with a few small boats on the slip, the other of the Mirror against the cliff – to my right as I entered. The little craft was but a temporary blemish in a pure, unadulterated mineral world. Over-calmed by photography the sea element held an apparently lake-like quality. It was not so in reality – I had to leave without sighting the church.

To my good fortune, along a bit off the lifeboat slip, a fisherman in anchored boat was concluding the first step in crab salad production – a step preferably left out of mind when ordering. My good fortune was not seeing things done to crabs but the immediate go ahead to row round the Lizard. The lucky chance of being in the right place at the right time in the right conditions was seized upon without delay. Before I had completed my heartfelt thanks to the crabber I was rowing with some gusto and an even measure of apprehension and excitement to the *Southern Cape*.

It was 12:30 when I set out for the Lizard. Half a mile on at Bass Point I started to take a long right-hander and entered an area of agitated sea. Large independent masses of water caused friction in coming together after being diverted by the great land obstruction. The Lizard is a point on a small scale map only — in reality it is two miles wide.

After a while I rounded a large leaning monolith — possibly the Lizard itself, although Bumble Rock appears on the map. It stood below the sunlit, white Lizard Light buildings. Before me was an awesome barrier of low lying jagged rocks stretching seaward. As I approached, all thoughts of threading my way between them evaporated. I angled Epic past the most southerly tip and was surprised to see a slip-way by the side of a small beach tucked away in Polpeor Cove. Conditions were perfect for a landing but I was psyched-up to reach Mullion Cove. I headed joyishly northish.

Sunburn and Intermittent Showers
(The Lizard to Porthleven)

Thankful that the weather had dealt me the kindest hand I hastened on, away from waters seldom so lenient. Off Kynance Cove I ceased rowing in time for the lunchtime shipping forecast. The 'light, variable' wind was eminently acceptable, and as far as 'fog around dawn' was concerned — I was not. I was happy bobbing about close to another Gull Rock and a Lion Rock — which looked like a lion, complete with sungoldened, lichened mane. The landscape I knew through the brushwork of other artists. At the time I had no wish to attempt a landing and commune with fellow man, for there at the bottom of England I savoured a personal high.

The painters' paradise slipped astern as I made use of the remaining favourable tide to row towards Mullion — five miles away. Two miles from my destination, as the tide began to run back to the Lizard, I was offered a tow. I declined, citing my particular masochistic bent. The considerate fisherman asked if I had been at sea in the vicinity of Kennack Sands the previous night. My far from convincing performance had been witnessed by the Lizard Coastguard — of which he was a member. Unknown to me my safe landing had been overseen. Without even an implied tut tut, the part-time lookout puttered off to Mullion Cove. Half a *mile* later I received another tow offer and a reminder of the increasing speed of adverse tide. I thanked boatman number two and said I would make haste under my own steam and keep close to the cliffs to avoid the strongest tide. After my recent experience, I should have been tenderly hugging the coast — out of the return ticket zone.

About the time I recrossed the fiftieth parallel I became aware that the top outsides of my calves were well done. I thought my legs were protected by a towel but when rowing in feet back mode, as opposed to legs straight out in front, my legs angled outwards to avoid contact with the oars — and so caught the slightly slanting rays. In the lee of a rocky outcrop I donned my dried jeans — belatedly bolting the door. Between the mainland and Mullion Island I sighted a group of buildings on a hilltop with others below by the sea. I still had a strenuous row before, at 4:30, Epic nonchalantly nudged the sand within the protecting arms of the harbour walls. It seemed more than twenty four hours earlier that I left Porthoustock.

A willing helper assisted in hauling Epic a few yards onto the newly washed sand. To the sound of children's *Swiss Family* and *Swallows* chatter I left to climb the grassy slope on the south side. From there, over the next half hour I saw the sand round Epic turned over by little feet as adventure was kindled in young minds. Between two tall pinnacled islets, just beyond the harbour, I spotted St Michael's Mount in the hazy distance. Below me, within the trodden circle, was my little ship — waiting to transport me to a real castle in the sky.

MULLION COVE

'—Epic nonchalantly nudged the sand within the protecting arms of the harbour walls.'

Returning to the beach I helped Bob, from whom the second tow offer came, to move some of his gear above the tide-line. There I fell over an outboard motor and sat down in evil smelling, mushy seaweed. That was but a small blip for fortune smiled immediately. After helping move my dinghy up the beach, Bob, a man of many showers, said for ten pence I could use the facility in his holiday camp. After a short walk up the hill I stood expectantly in a cubicle. My bag, clothes and towel festooned the door hook. Other accoutrements including a sample bottle of bright blue shampoo were crammed onto the small shelf. The reason for my having the world friendly shampoo—possibly blueberry and cucumber, was wholly the small bottle size. The hot caressing spray did not materialize. My ten pence had primed the mechanism in the adjacent cubicle. I transferred my impedimenta and then luxuriated beneath a hot refreshing cascade. In blue lather I eased away the muscular stresses of my fifteen mile row. What heavenly bliss for a while, and what a shame the water cutting off when my ten pence worth ran out—I must have thought. After rinsing myself and washing the smelly portion of my jeans at the sink, I set off wetly to Mullion village. There in an old inn—The Old Inn, I dined sitting on O S sheet 204—to protect the seat from my damp jeans.

It was darkish when I collected my sleeping bags from the boat and headed higher up the grassy slope to bed down—or perhaps up, for the night. Lying inside my bag—which was inside the orange plastic survival bag, I looked across at the lights stretching from Marazion to Mousehole, then left at the odd twinkle, then left again at the darkness that hid the empty Atlantic. I wondered if my voyage would end before I reached the Ocean. As the night progresses, darkness remained incomplete—a three-quarter moon oversaw the half-light. My burnt calf (the sacrifices one makes) was very painful as bag and I slipped gently down the slope. That was not a problem for the direction was not towards the cliff drop and obstructions ruled out a rendezvous with Epic. The plastic caused me to be wet and over warm at first, and later, wet and over cold as the light night advanced. I slept very little and was therefore able to periodically reach out and bring my painting bag down to my new elevation. Being fully awake at 4:30—thinking it was later, I took out my torch and radio, book and pen and was ready for the six o'clock forecast. Realising my pre-emption of the lark I tried to ignore the cold and *doze* in the dawn.

After warming my hands in the sea I stowed the torture-bed-bag and fitted the sails ready for hoisting. 'I should be so lucky', I noted. At 7:05, under a clear blue sky fringed with pastel peach, I rowed out of Mullion Cove on a flat, still sea. Gwennap Head—twenty miles away and three miles before Land's End, appeared invitingly peaceful in the early mist.

The low temperature had hardened the sun barrier cream but I was not tempted to forgo the *lock up the bolted horse* treatment to hand-backs and face. My legs were confined to jeans for a while. A loud roaring sound like heavy surf breaking on a beach turned out to be just that. The waves from an apparently flat sea were funnelled into Polurrian Cove where the breaker's sound rebounded from the cliffs. After breakfasting on Mars (out of this world), banana and water, I hoisted the wet sleeping bag up the mast. As I ate I wondered at the cause of a light disc on the glassy sea surface. There appeared no rational reason for the phenomena. The mystery was solved when a drip from an oar set the day-time moon's reflection scattering. Like the sun barrier cream my cold brain had to be coaxed into useful employment.

A landing at Church Cove II seemed possible till the last minute. Single, lolloping waves guarded against dinghy landing and a more precarious relaunching. Two dolphins entertained me for half an hour or so off the cove and into the next. I got no nearer than thirty or forty yards from their joyful cavorting. My photographic record of empty seas and occasional distant dots would give more satisfaction to Kodak accountants than to persons interested in big fish-like things.

Just after leaving the dolphins I took advantage of the calm conditions and explored a secret grotto-type place. It was situated at Pedngwinian, below a cliff—at the end of a little cape *where ambush war canoes might lurk*. It was 9:30 when I eased Epic into still water behind protective outlying rocks and glanced over the side. A shaft of sunlight penetrated the depths revealing, like a hologram, eerie subterranean green rocks. I leaned further for a better view and my heart *exploded*. From under the boat snaked a giant conger—I thought. The monster was in fact the reflection of an oar. As I tipped the boat the destorted reflection sprang onto the surface. I left for Porthleven—three miles further on, rowing past Gunwalloe Fishing Cove which marked the beginning of the three mile stretch of Porthleven Sands. Half way along the sandy beach, which at the time was mostly hidden below the high tide, is Loe Bar—which not surprisingly bars access to the Loe—a mile long lake leading towards Helston.

Previously when looking at the map I planned to step ashore at the Bar, push Epic onto The Loe and there peruse the wild-life and possibly paint. Armchair sailing has much to recommend it — getting wet and reality can be dispensed with. Looking at the Bar for real, I took into account its off-putting height which, had I been able to land safely, would have demanded expending a great deal more energy than is sensible on a hot sunny beach. A hazardous bar beaching would have been in total contrast to the peaceful, beer-garden landing executed at Tresillian during the previous voyage.

Rowing on to Porthleven harbour was quite strenuous work. The sea was slight but a little lumpy. That and an increasing onshore breeze made progress slow. I was pleased to pass the rocky shallows off the entrance and head down to the inner harbour under the protection of the long breakwater. At last I had passed the tall turreted church tower with its *afterthought,* stunted spire on top. It had been a tantalizing landmark for long enough. I tied up alongside steps — over and down from the Harbourmaster's office and went up and over to report. A sign at the office informed — Closed till Monday, so I went back over and down to Epic and moved her along to a metal ladder. Even with an absent harbourmaster it is not done to hog the steps. With my little boat tied to line, long enough to allow her to settle when the harbour emptied, I climbed the ladder which twisted disconcertingly — the single shackle fixing was, at most, economical.

On a cliff-ledge just north of Porthleven I sat looking across Mount's Bay waiting for the 13:55 shipping forecast. Predannack Head, six miles distant, was the last land visible to my left. Ahead, due west, with the distance down to fifteen miles, stood Gwennap Head. Before it and almost in line were the Logan Rock headland and Pedn-mên-an-mere — guarding the Open-air Theatre at Porthcurno. I listened to hear if a seafaring role was in the offing. 'North west three, occasionally four.' To the north-west at the top of the bay stood St Michael's Mount — I would play a waiting game.

Epic was to stay at Porthleven for a while. Robin would collect me in the early evening. I left the dinghy on the mud against the high harbour wall — which was twice the mast height, and set off to walk to Helston via The Loe. The three mile excursion was therapeutic. The type of dinghy journeying I was undertaking greatly exercised the mind. It was natural I suppose, that given half a chance, my legs would take the initiative when returned to land.

PORTHLEVEN

'I was pleased to pass the rocky shallows off the entrance and head down to the inner harbour
under the protection of the long breakwater.'

57

Foot followed foot, taking me along the fringes of the beautiful wave-less lake. Within an hour I passed the Coronation (QE II) Park Boating Lake — on the edge of town. It was at the time of that coronation, when very small, I was taken boating on a city lake. Sleek clinker rowing-boats with ropes attached to rudders on fine triangular transoms came to mind. I would not have thought then, that when big, I would have been weighing up the possibility of taking a smaller craft on an adventure to meet an ocean.

On the subject of little boats, I recall another episode from those early years in that same city — Birmingham. Standing on the pedals — unable to reach the seat, I propelled a grown-up's non-crossbarred, black bicycle to an indoor market. My mission was urgent. The road was wet following a downpour. Sunken tram-lines threatened to ensnare thin-wheeled traffic. Beware the gobbling, whining, rattling monsters. Treasure-chests — that had been ammunition boxes, lined trestle tables. Marbles, cap bombs, rubber balls and viewers with six scenes of London replaced the bullets. I coveted a set of four plastic sailing boats. Half a walnut-shell size with a slot for the flat plastic sail/mast, the shiny ships were recessed into a card. Pristine, red, blue, green and yellow, the fleet floated in the sink. I blew them and they fell on their sides. Inauspicious perhaps but also the start of a learning process. Lately I err towards under-canvassing. Several years were to pass before urges nautical returned.

I arrived in Helston at 4:45. After a quick walk round and a brief stop for a toasted tea-cake and mug of tea, it was time to return to Porthleven. I followed the road in case Robin chanced along. He had chanced earlier and was waiting for me at the harbour. Robin was in a rush and very hungry. So, while he drove the car down to the waterside at the inner end of the harbour, I descended the rickety ladder and rowed quickly to the slip where we transferred the boat contents to the car, tied oars, and mast wrapped in Bosun to the roof-rack, then carried the heavy, slightly water-logged Epic to the yard across the road. In no time, dormant taste-buds orgied as wrapped banquets from a local fish'n'chip shop were transferred to deprived stomachs.

'Dracula's Castle'

(Porthleven to Lamorna)

Six days later, the early forecast, ' . . . variable, decreasing three, occasionally four, fair, good'. My right leg had not healed after the roasting and there was little to take my mind off it as I queued impatiently in a St Austell bank. I glanced at the clock — 1300 hrs. I am not really superstitious but why not 1:00 pm. It was Friday the thirteenth. Earlier I had consulted my tide tables. High tide, 13:13 GMT. British Summer Time was one hour in advance, but the local tide correction was approximately minus one hour. Forgetting Friday superstitions and sunburn there was nothing preventing my return to Porthleven.

There was quite a swell running down the inside of the outer harbour wall. Epic rode over the surges and rocked confusingly, making rowing a faltering, slow business. When clear of the harbour I found the sea more ordered but quite choppy. The fresh wind was from the south — an onshore wind producing sharp little waves near the headlands.

Disused mine workings stood on the sloping cliff-tops — a manicured model landscape waiting for tin soldiers. From an empty sea there was no indication of scale. Engine houses and chimneys, one side bright with sunlight, punctuated the scene — children's building blocks in an uncluttered toy landscape.

By 4:00, Porthleven was just a smudge in the distance. Just a smudge — sorry Porthleven. A delicate, interesting smudge — as unlike a blot as it is possible to imagine. The temperature was just right — not too warm. 'The sky was mostly blue', I wrote in joggling waves, on joggling waves, and now read with difficulty from my notes. It took a little while longer to decipher the shaky, 'Hard to write' — possibly the most pointless statement ever penned.

It was extra choppy as I made my way with both sails set to starboard up to Cudden Point. I was watching surf breaking on the craggy outcrop when, '5:20 see St Micks'. Set against the hazy mainland, St Michael's Mount seemed small and rather understated compared with the nearer, darker rocks and white water. It was still, unmistakably, the most charismatic of Cornish landmarks.

For much of the next hour my gaze was on the Mount. Its mysterious form gradually dominated the background hills, and architectural details on the summit became more defined. Behind me, the distant dishes on Goonhilly Downs were visible in the clear air. Powerful and inspiring as the giant discs were they did not hold my attention for long. I looked ahead towards intriguing constructions that originated in previous centuries. When half a mile off, the island and grand castle/home still retained its mystery – partly because I approached the side shielded from the sun. Had I been in sombre mood, the scene may have taken on a sinister aspect. Dusk and a double bass, bowing sighing moans would have helped do the trick. After I had skirted to the left, the castellated towers with tall ornate chimneys appeared more cheerful – sunlight bathed the stone.

On the sunny-side in the lee of the harbour-wall I downed sail and rowed into St Michael's surprisingly large harbour. Towards the outer end of the harbour wall, to my right, I tied up close to a sturdy wooden ladder. From there a few minutes later I dropped my only jumper into the harbour. The previous year a couple who live on the Island called at my Gallery and invited me to drop in when passing – if you see what I mean. I called. They were out – but would be back at 9:00, before the causeway sank beneath the waves. I wandered over to Marazion from where I was impressed again by the majesty of the Mount, and mainland cod and chips. As the waters rose I re-crossed the causeway and called again at one of the terraced cottages behind the harbour buildings. I had a cup of tea and a chat with Richard and Maggie. They offered me a bed for the night, but I had to do what a man had to do. I settled for my wet woolly going in the drier. They must have wondered at such odd behaviour as I wandered from the cosy cottage into the pitch darkness. Wearing my warmly tumbled jumper I fumbled round the harbour and safely down to Epic.

Bagged and without the protective plastic I floated comfortably in Epic. I faced the Mount on which *Dracula's Castle* was floodlit. A film produced in Cornwall in the seventies depicted Mevagissey as Whitby and St Michael's, with little transformation necessary, became the vampire's Transylvanian haunt. The appearance of a crescent moon, bats flitting softly and my floating in a *ply-wood box,* did not quite transport me to Bram Stoker-land. In the absence of sighing moans I fearlessly drifted off – to sleep.

ST MICHAEL'S MOUNT

'Its mysterious form gradually dominated the background hills, and architectural details on the summit became more defined.'

I woke early to catch the forecast. It was a calm, clear morning. Later a force four to five wind might arrive from the south-west — that would rule out my heading towards Land's End. Such speculation could wait — I was going to look round the Mount. Not wishing to intrude into the silent island hamlet at such an early hour I mooched round the harbour end for a while, privileged to enjoy on my own the stillness and silent beauty of that majestic setting. Faint day noises began on the mainland. At 7:45 a Penzance helicopter droned off to the Isles of Scilly. The causeway/road was submerged more often than not — one reason why very few motor vehicles disturbed the peace on the Mount.

After marmalade on crumpets at the terrace cottage, Richard guided me round the gardens and buildings. The island seemed bigger when being explored. The seaward side, not usually opened to visitors, is more rugged than the sheltered, greener and more formal harbour-side. The half tamed, steep grassy sloped terrain with granite outcrops, incorporates secret stone and brick walled terraces. Bursting with varied foliage and scattered with urns and partly overgrown stone steps, it was a pleasing partnership by nature and man — no shaved lawns or tortured, topiaried plants.

I will not describe the fascinating, atmospheric interiors — you must walk the causeway or be taken by boat to see for yourself.

From battlements near the top of the buildings I looked down at the tiny Epic, way down below. There was no mistaking the Mirror tucked in by the left-hand side of the harbour entrance — she was the smallest craft and the only one with a sleeping bag at the mast-head.

Lord St Levan was further along the terrace changing a flag for a light-weight one — trying to induce a flutter in the almost still air. I was introduced, having been asked to address him as My Lord. Those working on The Mount addressed him likewise and were happy to do so — they liked and respected their Lord. He was interested in my project, having a personal interest in the small village of St Levan — just a mile from the last boat stopping place on the South Coast. Porthgwarra is the final bolt-hole, but only in good weather and for small boats. It was where I would have been happy to end my voyage — having taken Epic along the whole of the South Cornwall Coast.

My hosts and two other *crew* from the Mount boarded a boat as I left. Using my camera, the jovial band took a few photographs of me afloat in Epic. I am pleased to have the *evidence*. My own partial self portraits taken on the voyage, usually when feet-steering, show just feet and lower-legs interfering with the Cornish landscape.

At 11:30, as the helicopter returned from Scilly, I rowed away towards Penzance – two miles distant in a slight bluey haze. A faint breeze materialized and I raised the jib. It was soon joined by the Bosun to which I attached a handy length of springy elastic to use as a sheet. Wafting on I was annoyed by a buzzing jet-ski – 'bloody' was my notation. A single jet-ski, or droning outboard-powered *pleasure* craft, can ruin the peace for many. They should be baffled or segregated – be *hived* together. The Bosun's elastic stretched as the breeze increased, spilling the wind. I held the corner of the sail as the rising wind rushed me into a corner formed by the beach-end, piled with huge, angular granite hunks, and the harbour wall. The few hundred yards row to the harbour entrance was strenuously slow. I clawed my way to shelter into rapidly forming little waves – sculpted by the forecast wind from the forecast direction. Perhaps a more sensible sailor would have positioned himself upwind in anticipation and not found himself in a tight corner. A more sensible sailor would also have overlooked a piece of elastic when seeking a sheet.

Penzance harbour was pleasantly peaceful. The Scillonian had popped off to the Scillies. There was just enough bustle and pottering to give anonymity to my mini-cruiser. With Epic on a running line between the coast road – raised on iron legs, and a modest sailing boat, I climbed a ladder and stepped between the rails onto the pavement. The sun shone warmly. I felt carefree and happily strolled into the metropolis.

The town is graced with fine architecture of various styles. The main street, built on a hill and oozing character despite sabotage by retailers' tasteless signs, could so easily become a gem again. The plastic shop-front blight is ripe for salvation. From a cafe, up steps off a side street, I ordered a tuna sandwich and received an ample lunch – heavy with tuna and generously accompanied with fresh salad. Penzance is well bestowed with art galleries and antique shops but on that occasion I gave them a miss. My mission was gastronomic and my thoughts were beyond the lighthouse.

The south-west wind was stronger as I left Penzance at 4:00. Without trepidation I headed for Newlyn — just a mile away, containing possibly the largest fishing fleet in Britain. Arriving after an hour's trip I spent a while rowing round the harbour — hoping to find the Lenten Rose, a smaller than average fishing boat from Mevagissey. Newlyn was busy — boats were manoeuvring and berthing, taking on fuel and ice. I spied what I thought was Nick the Greek's boat at the top end of the harbour. It was a beautiful pea-green boat but not Nick's — who is no more Greek than Rupert, his crew, is a bear.

Rounding a more *lighthousey* lighthouse than the thinner Penzance one — a light perched on a Doric column, I headed onwards. Half an hour later I lay off old concrete workings — silos I expect, and in the lee awaited the forecast. A helicopter dawdled overhead as ' . . . Thames, Dover . . . ' was drowned. Fortunately I received the nub of the forecast, ' . . . occasionally four . . . thunder developing . . . isolated fog . . . ' If that is my kind of fortune it is fortunate there are few *unfortunatelys*.

Rain started to fall as I passed the big pink doors of Penlee Lifeboat station — a mile from Mousehole. It was still raining as I rowed into Mousehole Harbour wearing my yellow oilskin. My carefree and happy demeanour on arriving in Penzance had waned somewhat.

My outlook brightened as I edged Epic onto the harbour-bed. A shouted greeting from a couple on the quay-side came from the crew of Windsong — a twenty four foot, bright yellow sloop moored against the wall at the other end (south) of the harbour. They had visited Mevagissey in their boat a few days before and called at the gallery — having seen my ''Epic' Voyage' book in the window. We had chatted of things nautical and of painting. Cheryl was a painter and Brian taught navigation. A falling tide hastened their departure. They were heading west and left with a ''May see you later''.

The harbour was emptying so Epic was safe for a while. In the company of the artist and navigator I settled my harbour dues. ''Half a day, eleven foot, no charge''. Thank you harbourmaster. Divested of wet-weather gear we yarned salty tales in a nearby restaurant. Dining-chair sailing we found as easy as arm-chair sailing. They told me about their sailing down from the Isle of Man. After a couple of pints I found little problem in rounding Land's End and Cape *Hornwall*.

MOUSEHOLE

'It was still raining as I rowed into Mousehole Harbour wearing my yellow oilskin.'

Later, alone on my damp thwart, I found the prospect of doubling the Cape, as we mariners say, by no means cut and dried. I rigged running lines, from stem to harbour wall and back to boat, and stern to nearby punt and back to boat. It was a bit of a fiddle but made casting off while afloat a simple matter. One end of each line is released, freeing the boat—which ends up full of wet rope.

It stopped raining and the night started well. At 1:00 I lay down in my warm sleeping-bag, disregarding the earlier warning of thundery showers. Being afloat must compensate to some degree for the hard, uneven surfaces that I was able to sleep on. Exhaustion and minimal hours of sleep must also enter the equation. Floodlights at the harbour entrance and nearby street lights illuminated the scene. Ripples radiated from Epic as I extricated myself sufficiently from the bag to perform an undercover operation with the bailer. Feeling myself the target of hidden eyes I was relieved when re-zipped.

An hour later, no, not the bailer, rain fell on my unprotected bag. I willed it to stop. Minutes passed. My bag soaked up the fine rain. I willed and got wetter. Hurriedly I vacated my delightfully warm, snug, why didn't I take any bloody notice of the forecast, sleeping-bag, before it got too heavy to stuff into a polythene bag—where I should have been. Back in my damp oilskin, waterproof trousers and wellies, I waited for the dawn.

Because of the illumination I did not realize Sunday had sidled out of the gloom till I saw Windsong, not yet yellow, silhouetting towards the harbour exit/entrance. I made my way over to wave them off, feeling sure they would be surprised. Surprise was mine too, and a modicum of embarrassment, when I saw Windsong being strategically tied up nearer the entrance.

It could have been a mistake to accept the offer of breakfast on board Windsong for I was becoming excessively at one with nature. The cabin was dry and real *indoors*. Intimate may have been a boat vendors appraisal of the accommodation but to me it was palatial. The ability to muster hot rolls was a strong selling point. Warming tea and the baker's oven aroma had the edge on bananas and water at that early hour. Epic's little had a lot going for it though, including standing headroom and a purchase price less than a television set—which has access to fewer channels.

At 8:15, after shaking hands with the crew of the yellow sloop, I upped jib and rowed out of Mousehole Harbour. There was 'half cloud cover'. A clue to my slightly sombre mood. Had I not thought the voyage to be nearing its damp death throes I might have optimistically opted for, half blue sky. The early forecast from the Scilly station was ' . . . north-west by west, five'. Keeping close inshore I headed on towards Lamorna Cove — two and a half miles away. I was rushed along the coast under jib power, hoping the wind would behave for an hour. St Michael's Mount, distant with its top tower lost in low cloud appeared from behind St Clement's Island — positioned protectively a few hundred yards off Mousehole's harbour entrance. I supposed a heavyweight flag flapped behind the ominous stratus.

I assumed the half dozen or so wave-formed caves in the low, fractured granite cliffs — south of the village, was/were the Mousehole/s. Further along at the base of the ferny hillside that sloped down to the sea were mounds of sea-quarried blocks through which the surf surged noisily. There were a few off-lying rocks that broke the surface after the heavier swells receded. Epic headed out a little and raced on. For a second or two the light sun disc threatened to break through a blackened sky. The clouds closed then relented for a short while allowing swathes of brightness to move across the landscape. I put on my life-jacket as the north-west wind hurried me along even more swiftly.

Up to Carn-du — the headland protecting Lamorna Cove, the passage had been invigorating. Noticing a few small white buildings marking the Cove I attempted to head in. A wicked wind blew down the valley taking me on — away from Lamorna. My enforced heading would have taken me outside Tater-du — a little white lighthouse a mile away on the lower slope of the next promontory. I feared being swept back into wind blown Mount's Bay. I recalled the 'force five' and invigorating became frightening. In a precious lull, with great relief, I was able to claw down the sail, lash it and row into the protection of the granite cliffs. Safe and free from the wind I headed back towards the breakwater wall that at first seemed part of the shoreline. Areas of large quarried blocks adorned the hillside. One would think arrangements of natural materials would not jar, but the austere draping detracted from the landscape. There was ample craggy charm without additions.

The sun shone as I rowed round the arm of the jetty in calm water and settled Epic on the sand between a scattering of stones and mini-boulders. It was 9:30 and few people were in the beach/jetty area when I landed. Within five minutes a Japanese gentleman arrived and asked if he could take a picture of his three small children standing by the little dinghy.

I quickly de-masted and unloaded, leaving mast, oars and gear on the road-side in the protection of the helpful Bob—the car-park *sentry-man*. After moving a few stones, I pulled Epic a little way up the beach and hurriedly walked the half mile or so to the public phone-box, up the valley road. Julia had just left to man, *or lady,* the gallery. I had to wait till lunch-time to make arrangements for a lift home which gave me a few hours to enjoy Lamorna.

My photograph of the beached boat under a heavily overcast sky is a sad silhouette. Somewhere in Japan there is likely to be a picture I would rather have—three smiling children in front of a sunlit Epic.

The story could have ended at Lamorna. Many sound reasons for calling it a day were relegated by a growing obsession to round Land's End. Help was on hand to carry Epic up on to the jetty, beyond the reach of possible rough seas. My little boat would be safe while I was away waiting for favourable, gentle winds.

In the cafe, a step or two up from the beach, I poured tea-leaves into a cup while poring over the Land's End map. The clouds brightened and heightened revealing the distant Lizard. The penultimate leg was finished and the end of the whole voyage was nigh—only two folded map sections remained to be investigated. Had I looked in the tea-cup for a sign, there were leaves enough to suggest another volume. Later I would give more than a nod to the Lamorna Wink—the pub, ten minutes walk along the valley road. First I explored the woodland and tumbling stream that I had just passed alongside on my walk to the phone-box. Mild melancholia receded as, remembering to use the strainer, I had another cup of tea, then set off. The huge granite blocks round which the little stream rushed were cloaked in moss, adding softness to a sheltered scene—so unlike the hillside above the harbour. Nature was in the process of reclaiming artists' studios—creating glorious rustic compositions—mysterious tree landscapes—Lamorna Birches.

LAMORNA STREAM

'First I explored the woodland and tumbling stream that I had just passed alongside on my walk
to the phone-box.'

Pure Theatre

(Lamorna to Porthgwarra)

Three days later I returned to Lamorna Cove. Wind-less weather was probably imminent. Meteorology is not an exact science. How, whatever was bringing the *non-wind* would know when to stop I did not dwell on. At an early hour, from a camp-site a few miles from Mevagissey, I press-ganged my younger brother and his little yellow Rascal van. Michael would take me, *way down to La-morn-a.* My obsession to round the most westerly point of England and reach Sennen Cove remained healthy. (I have deleted the adjective, overwhelming—even after the event it seems a bit inappropriate.) Before heading west we undertook a leisurely loading. There was no rush. The distance between Lamorna and Porthgwarra where I proposed to wait for calm and a fair tide was only six miles.

Mentally and physically I felt in good order. There were people though who less readily accepted the first state. Over the last few years I had daily gone through a range of exercises lasting just a few minutes and using as many muscles as possible. The twisting, pushing and pulling included a *hoist the main-s'l yuh swabs* routine. With arms raised and fists clenched, one pushing down the other up, I slowly lowered them to my waist. I repeated the straining on imaginary rope with the lower fist on top. There was little effort employed raising sail on my boat but I had to be prepared for the unknown—and helping Epic round the End was certainly in that category. The hours of rowing over the preceding weeks, particularly the long row to Mullion, had given me confidence in my stamina—my calloused hands provided certification.

Friends told me of a couple who lived in Lamorna. He dived and it was suggested I look him up—to get the low-down on sea conditions in his area. With the van parked in the hedge, Michael and I visited the little granite cottage. We stepped down into a treat of retreats. A boulder strewn stream rushed through a secluded garden, bordered by wild, protective woodland. Keith and Christine were at home. Over tea, in the tranquil garden, my confidence was tested.

"You've done well to get this far . . . stick while you're ahead . . . risk . . . bad currents . . . " Keith's repeated warnings and suggestions that I go no further turned the interlude into a kind of last tea sermon. Later at the beach I was tying the oars to the cleats on the gunwale—with laces from my old running shoes. Keith looked on with disbelief. After a "Nobody would think less of you if you called it a day . . . " he asked me to phone when I reached my destination—which I took as encouragement.

It was warm and the sky was a high bright haze above a calm sea, textured with small rounded wavelets. With the Bosun neatly wrapped round the mast and the jib in the sail-bag, in accordance with my take it easy itinerary, I rowed westward. From the beach and later the cliff-top, Michael photographed Epic's progress. The pictures are the only photographic record of my voyaging not taken from Epic — excluding *cast-offs*. They are precious reminders of my time afloat, and I knew nothing of them till the trip was over. The first picture shows me in shirt sleeves plying the short non-matching oars. Against a background of granite cliffs, Epic looking quite diminutive is leaving Lamorna. A large white bucket stands on the transom seat. There is nothing to suggest ocean aspirations. The series ends with a *speck* — detectable under a magnifying glass. It is about a mile from the larger, full-stop sized Runnel Stone — a large rock a mile off Porthgwarra.

Lunch-time and ta-ta to Tater-du. Where would I be that time tomorrow? I mulled. Requiring local information, I gripped the oars and pulled towards the answers. An hour later a buzzing diversion to seaward interrupted my thoughts. A large dolphin was leading two men in a small rubber dinghy in mutual entertaining. While I was escaping the dreaded combustion-engine it seemed the single sociable mammal was seeking them out. The dolphin dived and the dinghy-men disappeared to the east.

As I closed the shore a fleck of white became a gable-end on one of the few buildings in the fishing hamlet of Penberth Cove. A *giant-gateway* — like a huge black H on its side was a mystery at the time. It turned (not recently) out to be a defunct capstan. A mechanical winch now hauls out the boats. Anchored offshore was a solid little open fishing-boat named Lily. While the stocky fisherman was waiting to have his boat winched up the granite slip — constructed on an exposed beach between large boulders, I chatted to him. In such calm conditions landing at Porthgwarra should be no problem. I left Lily to be hauled out and join the rest of the fishing boats — about a dozen in all, at the top of the beach.

Soon two dolphins came to keep me company for ten minutes or so. (Perhaps dolphins believe three's company.) On looking round I was surprised to find them close to the bow. Wing mirrors are a serious consideration. I was reminded of the dolphin that greeted me, in an ignoring sort of way, at the other end of Cornwall when I left Plymouth Sound two years before. I hoped the portent would not be similar — an hour or two after that first sighting I was nearly shipwrecked. Three miles on I would take a sharp right-hander into the Atlantic.

After passing the tall, jagged topped Logan Rock ridge — a formidable landmark that juts into the Channel, I was surprised to hear a sound more like distant clapping than surf against granite. Looking behind I noticed what appeared to be a large patch of red and white flowers on the cliff-top. The sound was repeated and the mystery solved. Applause — but not for me. The floral arrangement synthesized — became an audience enjoying Twelfth Night (I learned later) at the open-air Minack Theatre — Porthcurno.

If boating be the food of fun, row on.

Wouldst thou not wonder at such coincidence.
Neither knew I by title the enactment played,
nor that I thithered whence from mine dozenth night
alone with noblest Epic.

Slow exit — stage starboard.

Rowing against the tide for a further hour positioned me off Porthgwarra. Relieved that I noticed the slipway — a lighter scar in the granite, I headed in to the last refuge. The tide had unfortunately just covered the sand in the channel. A line fixed to the lower end of the slip and leading seawards was a great help when landing on the immense *cobblestones*. There was little scraping of hull as I hauled Epic from the minimal surges. After unloading, a bearded chap helped me lug Epic a few yards up the granite slip. The macho non-stop lift pre-empted a hurried release on to a lumpy projection. I winced inwardly. Not wishing to seem ungrateful I left checking the thin ply till later.

A handful of persons, mooching, lolling or lying and four fifteen foot fishing boats drawn onto the slip, was the whole sea side action of *Down-town* Porthgwarra. A tunnel led to *Up-town*. The seaward end has a strange, non-accessible, higher second entrance. In mining times, St Just dynamiters had blown a way through the cliff to facilitate the carting away of seaweed. Their explosive ability cannot be questioned but a D for direction would be over generous.

The *Shed-café*, sheltered away near the top of the slip, was closed by the time I made my way there. In the vicinity I conversed with a gentleman, a few years my senior, in my quest for local knowledge. Eric turned out to be the author of children's books, the cafe and harbour master and one to direct me to a seasoned fisherman. Les, skipper of one of the small boats, lived two uphill miles away at Trethewey. Before I had walked a mile I was offered a lift by the bearded one. He was, or had been, a merchant-seaman and obviously more used to steel-plate than plywood constructions. Peaceful Porthgwarra was his family's favourite spot and he was taking them home after a relaxing visit. My arrival, fortunately, had been quiet and relatively unobstrusive.

PORTHGWARRA

'Relieved that I had noticed the slipway – a lighter scar in the granite, I headed into the last refuge.'

I soon found the man of local knowledge. He invited me into his home where he delivered the goods. He intended to go to sea himself the following day and was fairly sure conditions would be favourable. The completion of the voyage, as my walk back to the cove, seemed all down-hill. I strolled through a rugged landscape shaped by strong winds. Sparse, tortured trees were testament to prevailing winds. It was a landscape draped at times with damp mists. Happily, my descent was through countryside wrapped in quiet summer.

Back at Porthgwarra I stopped to admire a vigorously carved stone relief. Set above the doorway it graced a fine granite cottage set back from the sea. The large headed, open mouthed fishy monster was apparently a dolphin – a rather unkind representation. A gentleman, seated in the porch toasting the fine evening with a glass of good cheer on ice, had no objection to my photographing the beast. I wondered at the local significance. There was none – the heavy carving had been transported from *up-country* by a previous owner. Noticing my sun-parched appearance, the kindly John offered refreshment. I gratefully accepted and thoroughly enjoyed a tasty iced beer.

At the slip I filled the hull damage with plastic-wood. The plywood structure had been broken and though the break was almost closed, the fracture needed sealing to prevent seepage, waterlogging, and to restore peace of mind. With information from the knowledgeable Les I felt confident that my imminent challenge would be successful. Up-town, I checked out the other amenity, closing the phone-box door behind me.

''If you're at a loose end I'll drive you over to the pub.'' I had rung Keith to let him know I arrived safely. I was at a loose end and happy to be so, but there were fifteen hours of countdown remaining, and, well, I have my weaknesses. The evening was still and the sea was beautifully, boding well, flat. A large seal made its way into the inlet, surfacing tentatively. It raised its huge square head to con and sniff out invaders. I lay and watched the gentle wildlife, happily at one with the world, waiting to be taken to a pub. Life was good.

After a last sup in the First and Last pub – Sennen, I was returned to Porthgwarra. The bright headlights flashed their way back to Lamorna leaving me in darkness, groping my way down to Epic. The slip slope was really too steep for sleep, by the seashore, but I gave it a try. I moulded myself to coincide with the undulations of the large smoothed blocks of granite and cement infill. I got in the groove in an area a few yards above the tide line and below the boat. I used my trainers to combat the worst projections and the polystyrene block was utilized to arrest the slipping sleeping-bag. Neither ploy was too successful. My iliac-crests – side pelvis tops, would not be comforted. The inexorable slide I counteracted by continually up-wriggling – feet pushing against crevice or bump.

Throughout the night I was lullabied unsuccessfully by the rhythmic slow swishing of small waves on soft sand. In the early hours I heard a perturbing sound akin to munching of thick seaweed stems by powerful jaws — a mystery. It came out of the blackness — from the sea, a couple of dozen yards away. Bats, which I assumed dwelt in the tunnels, were a pleasant diversion.

My sleeping-bag, although it had wandered somewhat, stayed warm. From the comforting interior I noted, '5:55 Thur 19 Aug', local areas were forecast to be 'variable or variable south west, three or less'. Oh yes. 'Possible fog later.' Fog later did not concern me at the time — the present was very much on my mind. The sea, just three yards from my bag, was still calm. It was all systems go. My instructions were to leave at about 10:30. The remainder of the outgoing tide would take me to Land's End and the turning tide would take me round. It was as simple as that.

There was time to kill. I had a lie in and watched scurrying, inch long, marine woodlice type creatures. They were a lighter, taupey colour and more feelery than the compact, shiny garden type. They remained outside the bag I am pleased to say. The grey head of the seal appeared close in. Perhaps it was a vegetarian and had been there all night. Had I occupied the blubbery one's sleeping area? Hopefully not, for it was better equipped than I to cope with the inclined, lumpy bed.

Before 7:00, a lady swimmer aged seventy (she told me) came down to the cove to swim. Soon after, with the aid of gravity, Les launched his boat with a rush. The steel-shod keel ran true down the iron stained groove. With his white mock-clinker boat hitched to the rope that I found so handy, the knowledgeable fisherman prepared for sea. Down-town Porthgwarra was a hive of activity. I left to walk up and over Gwennap Head — to see what lay in store.

On my way to the cliff-top I looked down into the cove. Epic, listing towards me hiding her white top-sides did not enhance the rugged beauty of the scene. The rectangular plan presented only varnished ply — displaying all the charm of a cheap wardrobe. The tide was going out. Clear sea just covered gently shelving sand. Several yards out the colour became light egg-sheil blue-green, then gradually darkened. When near the top of the headland I became aware of a sound like distant traffic noise. The volume increased. I reached the cliff edge and looked down. The sight blew my mind. To the east the sea held mill-pond qualities. Before me, hell boiled. The swells, the end product of an earlier Atlantic storm, rose up then sucked at the granite as the massive weight of water forced its way back into the turmoil. Tortured water tumbled down through the turquoise, churning out skeins of white warning that lingered on the surface.

Heading towards the H M Coastguard, Gwennap Head Lookout Station, I passed a *flock* of twitchers. There were male, female and young crouched close to the cliff edge with eyes to telephoto-lenses. Overlooking the empty sea to the south they remained motionless — statues overseeing the passage of time.

Following the cliff path I soon reached the lookout which was unmanned — for reasons of economy I suppose. If the bird watchers remained on station for a few hours they would notice if I rounded the headland as a species in danger. I walked on across the headland hoping to glimpse the Longship's Lighthouse which stood on a reef a little over a mile off Land's End. It was just over three miles away — hidden by a fog or mist that restricted visibility to a mile or so. During the previous few days I wondered if I would reach the most westerly point and pass by the Longships. It is as well I did not see the final sea-mark on that occasion. Turbulent seas, poor visibility and an empty lookout were quite enough to test my resolve.

On a large rock in front of more white ocean stood a bird with casual, ruffled feathers. Larger than a pigeon, it was brown and had something of owl and chicken about it. Before I had time to snap, it dipped out of sight. (Snap as in photography — *tetherwise,* I was surprisingly near the beginning.)

On a springy floral carpet I walked back to the cove. Rich, random patterns equalled the subtlety of antique Persian harmonies. Heathers of fiery purple-reds and burnt orange left little room for the spongy grasses and intense yellow gorse flowers. On reaching the twitchers, I noticed one of the number had ceased his vigil but remained sitting with the group. I quietly approached, bent over and whispered to him.

''What are you looking for?''

''Birds.'' He said, with a hint of hesitation that suggested he was not one hundred percent certain of my sanity. I slipped away without mention of the chicken-owl.

GWENNAP HEAD

'Rich, random patterns equalled the subtlety of antique Persian harmonies.'

The End and Beyond with the Great White
(Porthgwarra to St Ives)

From Porthgwarra phone-box I rang Falmouth Coastguard, informing them of my proposed destination. They wished to know what safety equipment I was taking. It was a serious business.

"Distress flare, fog-horn, compass, life-jacket, warm jumper and waterproof." I replied.

"Contact us when you reach Sennen Cove."

"I will." An adrenalined auto-pilot answered.

"Good luck." A cool, professional voice ended the communication.

At launch minus ninety minutes I left the phone-box. Les brought his boat back in. Eric helped him winch it up the slip. I watched and chatted then wandered up to the shed/cafe with the winch-man/harbourmaster who changed roles and opened early. After teas Eric inscribed his children's adventure book for me. I was pleased to receive the gift – rich with happy-ever-afters, it was an ideal talisman. To sustain me on my journey he insisted I take a pasty. The pasty was large, pale, heavy and most welcome for I was low on victuals. Later he helped carry Epic down onto the sand. I decided to take a photograph of Epic with the master-of-trades on the slip behind. I safely made my way over the rocks on the left side of the inlet. Returning I managed to fill both wellingtons with sea. Wet feet did not turn to cold. The countdown continued. Kindness shown that day ensured a relatively relaxed period with little butterfly activity.

The time arrived. I eased Epic into the water and boarded in the lunging sort of way that keeps her upright. Hurriedly locating the oars in the rowlocks I took the skin off the middle joint of the little finger on my left hand. That would not have mattered normally but the little wound caught my jeans as I rowed and in a few strokes had streaked them with blood. Man-eating sharks, or sharks eating men, are almost unknown that close to land. A happy state, helped no doubt by the rarity of blood-stained offerings. The launch was far from perfect but I was half an hour ahead of schedule.

The seal raised his large head and saw me off—wishing me the best of riddance no doubt. He was close enough to be photographed but as I pressed the button he sank. (The whiskery white tuft is difficult to spot in my picture.) A hundred yards out I stopped to take stock. Epic rose soothingly over the slight swells. I squeaked off my wellingtons, wrang out my socks and placed them on the stern seat to dry. From the lidded ice-cream box I took my new Swiss Army knife and cut a square of Elastoplast—to protect my little digit. It seemed fitting that the tool sporting a red cross logo should be first used for such a purpose. With teeth and both hands occupied and the sharp blade in intimate proximity with my nose, I watched the heavier, more streamlined starboard oar slip silently overboard. It was reassuring to see the fail-safe system at work. From the trainer lace that held the rowlock to the cleats the long boot-lace was attached, and to that, the oar was tied with a quick-release half bow. The wayward oar was tethered. Had Eric and Les been watching through binoculars they may have doubted my suitability for the job in hand. I retrieved the oar. Over wet jeans I pulled wet wellies—protection against sun-burn. (I obviously had no intention of swimming any great distance. Setting my feet in concrete blocks would also have shielded my feet from the sun.)

Porthgwarra seemed very familiar as I rowed away, particularly Down-town where few others, I imagine, have slept. The low rocky cliffs on the right of the Cove stretch south for two or three hundred yards, ending at Hella Point—providing protection from the west. Over the end of the outcrop rolled breaking waves. There was less swell and white water the previous day. I gave the Point a wide berth and rowed into the Atlantic Ocean.

A somewhat confused sea greeted me. Had I not taken my early morning stroll it would have been a more than somewhat confused mariner rowing out beneath the twitchers' gaze. Just a few hundred yards out from the cliffs I was spared the sight of the churning confusion. My eye-level being only thirty inches above the surface meant I viewed only the waves in contact with the cliffs. The roar of the scouring swells was to accompany me for some time. At first the sea surface was smooth with small rounded waves going my way—what I would have expected after two windless days. I headed towards the mist.

In what seemed no time, the sea behind me was empty. I was rounding Gwennap Head, I thought. Looking astern I was perplexed to notice a string of low lying rocks gradually rise up to form the one hundred and fifty foot high Logan Rock promontory. The swells were so long that I did not realize Epic was taking an imperceptible switchback ride.

I rowed out further intending to continue half a mile or so off the indented coastline. With the help of the tide I made good progress but was soon a mile out. I angled back in towards the barely visible Armed Knight — a rugged formation about a hundred and fifty yards long and standing that distance offshore. The defiant islet in what is usually a most inhospitable location for any type of shipping was just a mile and a half away. I knew it well — in two dimensions. It was depicted on the cover of the Land's End O S map, portrayed clearly on a blue sea but without the misty mystery I encountered. I had fantasized of taking Epic through the gap.

Ahead and behind, headlands receded and were swallowed by the fog. I passed through an area of short, sharp, non-breaking little waves that caused a bumpy ride for a while — perhaps Epic was passing through shallower water. At about 10:30 I sighted white water breaking on the Longship's Reef. The lighthouse, well over a hundred feet tall, remained obscured till I was nearly abeam. After thousands of miles of free reign the ocean's progress had been obstructed. Growing swells stampeded, forming huge waves that broke on the low reef barrier. I could detect three or four breaking waves in a half mile long line. A two hundred yard wide block of surf to the left, as high as the tower, hung for a moment then faded.

Passing between the Armed Knight and the mainland was no longer on my agenda. I could barely distinguish the slightly darker form of the off-lying island. My earlier view from the cliffs was encouragement enough to keep me equidistant between the Longship's Reef and the dangerous confusion that lay close in. I had reached the end of Cornwall.

LAND'S END

'I had reached the end of Cornwall.'

In a charged state of euphoria, I wrote in shaky hand:-

10.48 ROAR of Longships !
huge rollers !!
continuous ROAR
~~10.5~~ 10.52 Lands
End.

Half an hour later I turned right and Epic brushed through bands of foam. On diminishing swells I rowed through the Tribbens — a two hundred yards wide channel formed by the Cowloe rocks. Heavy waves crashed over the offshore barrier that gave protection to Sennen Cove's open harbour. I became aware of an odd and somewhat disconcerting phenomenon — the ocean's flow backed up behind the Cowloe and remained at a higher level. It seemed it must roll on like a tidal-wave. It did not — those thousands of tons of water remained, seemingly defying gravity.

To seaward the mist drew back. Sunshine and blue sky appeared as if on cue. Perfect choreography — the last reel was nearly run. The roaring sounds of the sea faded as I approached the seaweed draped low lying foreshore. It stretched further than usual due to an exceptionally low tide. There was still over an hour till low water and the fingerings of weed and rocks would stretch a little further seaward and enclose more of the shallow *lagoon* at the end of the new lifeboat slip-way. After a final pull on the oars I crouched in the stern and Epic, bow up, glided over the clear shallow water on to the smooth concrete slip.

It was over. I was safe, and floated in a heightened happy state, bursting with relief. I had programmed into a world where taking the tide to Sennen was admissible — where thoughts of anything but a routine boat trip was not. My self-appointed taskmaster had resided long enough — he slipped from my shoulders as I stepped ashore at journey's end.

Sennen Cove was quiet. A few people sat at the top of the beach by a fleet of hauled out boats — some distance away. A solitary child was building castles. Was it St Michael's he conjured from the sand? If so, I hope he had a paper flag that would fly from the top turret — with or without the wind.

The Sennen lifeboat was moored a couple of hundred yards off-shore — so I hoped not to have to move the dinghy in a hurry. I strode up the slip and found the winch gear being overhauled inside the lifeboat station — I was free to phone and take refreshment. After informing Falmouth Coastguard of my safe arrival I ordered tea and sat at a table across the road from the cafe, next to the lifeboat station — it was almost continental. Holiday-makers sat at other tables. I felt on holiday too and removed my wellingtons to flex my white feet in the sunshine. My damp jeans and shirt, that retained the perspiration of my endeavours, dried in the glorious sunshine. I had luxuriated in my freedom for just half an hour when I found myself in conversation with a fisherman.

"Is a passage to St Ives possible in a small rowing boat?" I asked, wondering whether a future North Coast adventure was on the cards. At that moment I had no intention of continuing the voyage.

"Nearly five hours of favourable tide left . . . "

Being a spring tide with one of the greatest ranges of the year, it was therefore one of the swiftest. Less than twenty miles — four miles per hour, less two — courtesy of the tide — no problem. I strode back down the slip at 12:20 to pop round to St Ives. It was unrealistic to expect to row to St Ives in five hours. It was not the most sensible decision I had ever made. In mitigation I can say time was of the essence. My hurried foolishness allowed no time for what-ifs or a call to the coastguard. I confess to complete irresponsibility.

During my fifty minutes stay at Sennen Cove I did not stray far from the lifeboat station. That remote haven deserves better.

A few yards out to sea, while re-adrenaling, I swapped wellies for flip-flops, tied on my life-jacket and pulled the cord of my floppy white hat under my chin. Aire Point, a mile away at the far side of Whitesand Bay was obscured by mist — a warning, but I was already blinded by adventure. Leaving the great expanse of light sand that swept into the mist a respectful few hundred yards to starboard, I made haste. Large rounded swells that were soon to break on the beach passed under Epic. The squealed delight of hardy bathers, shepherded into a safe zone by life-guards, reached me above the sound of breaking surf as I headed quickly north.

The sun became lightly veiled. The distance between the tops of swells increased from ten to hundreds of yards as I propelled Epic obliquely away from the beach. Rowing conditions were perfect. My afternoon was mapped out. With the course set, I set about expending the necessary energy to meet my deadline. Relieved of making major decisions for a while, my mind turned to refuelling the body. I took a couple of mouthfuls from my gallon water bottle. This was repeated several times every hour to counteract dehydration. Hollow feelings from my neglected stomach prompted thoughts of the *great white*. The Porthgwarra pasty had remained solidly in place — tucked below my right-hand rowlock on the side-deck. Cool and very large, it was the ace of snacks — a king-size, a Henry VIII. With the oars sticking out in rest mode — held by my under-knees, I bit off the first instalment. In the time taken to place a pasty on the side deck I was plying the oars again, savouring a bite from the end pastry and eagerly awaiting the turn of the vegetables. Pasty eating, as well as providing sustenance has lottery excitement. You never know when you will hit the jackpot. In lesser pasties, meat may be a mere token. In all encounters there is the thrill of the gamble — even if at the end of the rainbow you find only turnip.

From the shelving sea-bed, one mile south-west of Cape Cornwall and five miles on from Sennen, rise twin islets. They appeared out of mist like volcanoed South Sea Islands. A glance at the map and the scale and name of The Brisons, if not their detail, became clear. They rose no more than fifty feet from the ocean. White water appeared to the land-side of the peaks. Because of the mist and my low vantage point I could not tell if the infrequent waves broke against Cape Cornwall — topped by a distinctive old mining chimney, or somewhere in the channel. The tide was taking me into the risky unknown. A healthy panic aided an about turn and I rowed out to sea — away from the problem islets. The Cowloe phenomenon pertained at the Brisons — only more-so. As I rowed up towards the ridge I became aware of the extent of the breaking waves on the seaward side. A long detour was required. When away from the breaking seas I headed north again, pulling through an area of *shark-fin* wavelets — the result of back-wash from the islands. They were more troublesome than those encountered just south of Land's End and I was relieved when I finally bashed through.

My detour had taken me as far west as I had been off Land's End. If all went well I would be able to head between north and east till I reached St Ives Bay. At a respectable rate of knots I continued, leaving a healthy mile between Epic and the mist-shrouded cliffs. That rugged area of West Penwith is richly scattered with mining remains. The mist thickened and I was unable to detect the disused engine houses in the area around Botallack.

SENNEN COVE

'A few people sat at the top of the beach by a fleet of hauled out boats —'

When approaching the sturdy lighthouse-topped Pendeen Watch headland, three miles on from Cape Cornwall, I lost sight of land. The Sennen Cove fisherman had warned me to keep clear of the Three Stone Oar — one large and two tiny rocks, six hundred yards north of the Watch. From the lidded ice-cream box I took my compass, and with map in hand worked out my navigating strategy — fifteen minutes north-east then east till I sighted something. Loosing visual contact with Cornwall while heading towards the unseen Oars was not too disturbing. Trusting my little compass was — my instincts told me I was heading for Canada. I sipped water, took a bite from the *great white* and rowed quickly towards the patch of fog indicated by the compass needle.

My ten minutes in the fog seemed longer. The faintest of headlands materialized exactly where it should have been. The light-tower confirmed I was abeam Pendeen. A few hundred yards off the starboard bow the sea broke white against the Three Stone Oar(s), revealing the troublesome rocks which, unlike the Brisons, are low lying. My blind, faultless piece of navigation lasted long enough to give me confidence in the clever little compass, which unerringly pointed the way — knowing nothing of fog, fear or Canada.

Visibility to the west remained hazy. I headed into sunshine on a dark blue sea under a clear, pale blue sky. Had I been travelling the other way I would have been aware of the onset of wind sooner. Concentrating on brisk, purposeful rowing I failed to notice the changed sea surface — textured by wind formed junior waves. Tide and oars had been taking me towards St Ives at around five miles per hour and it was not till a pasty pause that the welcome, favourable breeze became apparent. It must have been three-ish, with Pendeen Watch still powerfully present about two miles astern, when I set the sails goose-winged — one each side of the mast.

Epic made respectable progress. No quicker than rowing but a welcome relief and a bonus to have my hands free — I was adept at feet steering by that stage. The motion was gentle and I took pictures of waves breaking at the base of the cliffs. There was no safe landing place before St Ives — it was imperative to keep up the pace. The wind eased. I row-sailed for ten minutes wondering if I could remain on schedule. The breeze returned to its previous strength and I willed away the miles.

The wind, still from dead astern, increased a little and Epic surged on with the boat-hook holding the Bosun out to starboard — to catch more of nature's favourable draught. Not long after resuming proper sailing, my next objective, Gurnard's Head hove into view — two miles away. The irregular, chunky outcrop did look like a gurnard's head. The headland and a few small off-lying rocks caused the racing tide to throw up huge plumes of sun-whitened surf. I took pictures as I sped by. My antics — seeking the best view between sail and gunwale, caused Epic to tilt and yaw. The resulting series of photographs records the boat clutter, sails and sky, a blood streaked jean-leg and a Gurnard's eye peeping over the gunwale. Success in one clear shot — Headland and White Plumes, is a powerful reminder of that frantic race for safety.

Four inlets further on I passed by Pendour Cove — to the west of Zennor Head. The association of Zennor and a beautiful Mermaid could be just a myth. You never know, perhaps if I had summoned the siren politely — 'Please myth . . . '

Dividing a passage into sections gave me a good idea of progress. Between Sennen and St Ives I sectioned thus: — Cape Cornwall — Pendeen — Robin's Rocks (half a mile before Gurnard's Head with no obvious ornithological attributes) and at the four/fifths mark — The Carracks, a large off-lying low rock which at the time was surrounded by crashing surf.

'4:00 The Carracks ½ ml. ahead?' The question mark was a sign of disbelief — had I really made such good progress? ''I am flying . . . stormy waters . . . '' I sang with gusto. Alone on the ocean, in a pushing-my-luck sort of way, I continued singing voyage-ending songs to ease away apprehension. There was white, patchy high cloud and sunlight sparkling the waves behind Epic. To have that magnificent arena to myself was unexpected. Other than two canoes and a small fishing boat off Sennen Cove, I sighted no other vessel at sea after leaving Porthgwarra.

I reeled in the remaining headlands and then, AND THEN, from behind Clodgey Point slid The Island — St Ives Head. Like man, it is not an island — although I have felt a certain affinity at times. My vision was just a tiny bit blurred — perhaps the effect of the beautiful breeze. That moment was the high point of highs. A chest heaving, teeth-clenched-grinning, euphoric pinnacle of elation. Yes, yes, yes.

4.30 *The Carracks* I can't believe it !!!! I scribbled.

With sails set to port I headed in towards Porthmeor Beach, where I saw the site, but could not pick out the hotel – The Garrack, from where I produced the oil painting (mentioned earlier). I sailed alongside the isthmus, two hundred yards off the crowded sandy beach. Had it been four months later my euphoria may have brought on a poem. As predicted, by 5:00 when I rounded The Island, the tide lost its easterly way. Had I dallied I would have faced a tide against wind situation. Short steep waves would have prevented progress and the tide would have taken me back. Back, wetly, to darkness and the Gurnard.

Off the harbour entrance I pulled down the sails and tidied up. On the hill overlooking Porthminster Beach stood St Ives Bay Hotel. Before being elevated to assistant chef in the hotel over the hill, I spent a few weeks there washing up alongside Felix – who hailed from Madrid where his family ran a restaurant. When Felix arrived, his English was a mere smidgen better than my Spanish which encompassed little more than, adios amigo. Within a few days our reciprocal tuition had equipped us to sing Davy Crocket together – using each others language.

I rowed into the harbour and tied up halfway along the Lighthouse Quay. Wind driven, frothy off-white spume engulfed Epic in that corner. She appeared set in meringue. Hardly a just desert – an ignominious resting place for the game little craft that danced over miles of pristine ocean.

While waiting for a lift home, I stood for a while by the slip near The Sloop Inn. Now and then a surge would swish over the harbour road soaking shoes and socks of the unwary and giving immense pleasure to one mischievous young boy. He stood nonchalantly in the danger zone till the last second, when he leaped away, enjoying his victim's embarrassment. Little sod.

Carefree and lost in nostalgia I whiled away a relaxed hour in the Sloop. Characters I took to be knowledgeable local fishermen I totally ignored.

ST IVES

'I rowed into the harbour and tied up halfway along the Lighthouse Quay.'

The yellow van duly arrived on the quay alongside Epic. With gear loaded, Michael drove to the slip while I rowed my last few strokes of the voyage. On a big swell Epic was swept high up the slip — a few yards from the Sloop. *Inn-keeping* to the end. I stepped out dry-shod and with Michael's help carried Epic a little higher up — out of the surge's reach. After sponging away the *meringue* residue we lifted Epic on top of the Rascal, then drove away.

The previous few days had been *oar-inspiring* but the euphoria could
not remain. My adventure slipped into history as I changed
down, synchronised with the regular world and became
a passenger in a small yellow van. Hayle was to port
— now left of course, when I said to Michael,
''I've just rowed round Land's End''. I knew
he knew, and knew I knew he knew, but I
still mentioned it a few more times
before arriving home. It is not
every day you can say you
have just rowed
round Land's

End.

Postamble

My log-book received just two more entries. One line five days after journey's end, 'Shivered when I got photographs of Brisons back.' Then a week later, '. . . callouses on my hands with ragged white edges − a reminder.' Though seventeen months have passed my mind retains, tattooed, those memories. In the meantime I again oar-hardened my palms on a third adventure with Epic. Before that, under a metaphorical bridge, disturbed and threatening waters flowed − causing me to wonder if I would ride with Epic again.

A few days after the last entry I felt twinges in my back. One day later I lay prone, in great pain with sciatica. "Exercise." "Do not move." Medicine is not an exact science. Never a casual user of pain killers − I pay the price for one too many. It was different then − I urged the creeping clock hands on to temporary relief. As days turned to weeks I counted the minutes between each big red pill. Perhaps forced exercise would have helped. By the time I hobbled, doubled, to a physiotherapist, the nerve-gripping pain had conquered my left leg and the big toe was devoid of feeling and motive power. Full recovery would take some time − as I am finding out. The cause of the bother, I am sure, was my rowing in a sciatic nerve disturbing posture. Over many hours I had forced an opening pressure on the vertebrae in my lower back. Had I performed while rowing, periodic back-straightening, I may not have become a temporary, red pill junkie. More importantly, I may have avoided the worrying times that followed.

That October, when I was able to walk in near human mode, Julia, Edward and I set off for two weeks, *you can't afford not to go at the price,* Turkey sunshine. My convalescing started on the right lines − a relaxing train ride to Reading. Then was set back a week − hanging on to a wire partition in a goods-van, Gatwick bound, for two hours. The flight was not the ideal precursor for a four hour coach-ride. When self-powered mobility is history, the spindley femurs of package flyers will no doubt be hinged. Towards the end of the first week a Turkish doctor was called to my bedside in the early hours. A chest pain rendered my breathing increasingly difficult. The September *lie-in* may have been instrumental in my condition. An injection and hey-presto − a week later I was able to undertake the return travel triathlon.

The first week of the new year had not expired when I experienced a repeat of *Turkey-chest* — but not so extreme. I was able to transport my complaint to the local surgery — for analysis while symptoms remained.

"Don't worry but you have just had a heart attack." A little later an ambulance medic — a young man whose name only I have forgotten, reassured with professional calm as he wired me to monitors and fitted an oxygen-mask. Through tinted windows, I looked with some emotion across St Austell Bay and down to Pentewan. I picked out the old gallery, then grassy banks and trees sped past the darkened screen.

There was a little pain and anxiety for a couple of days. Investigations followed — X-rays and scans. A screen showed my heart at work. The operative, as he edited the video for the specialist, said the pulsating organ looked in fine condition. A lighter piece of workings kept creeping into the picture.

"What is that?" I asked.

"That's your lung."

"Would it help if I kept it out of the way?"

"Please, if it's no trouble." (Or words to that effect.)

Shallow breathing and my lung remained out of shot. I could not resist one more deep breath. *The Return of the Lung* was an unnecessary addition — the heavy breathing bit part was deleted. A possible blemish on a chest scan was slowly traced on a distant screen. I could not breath it away.

"It may not be anything." Medicine is not an exact science. " . . . blood thinning drip in case."

Partial freedom a few days later — carrying a portable pump — a spaceman — small steps. Arrival of hot-food cabinet — high spot between blood tests. Intercept — lunchtime minus food and counting. Wheeled to the big scanner — tracked into tube — flashing lights circled clockwise, green and red. End of the tunnel — cool shepherds-pie, peaches and custard.

One week later — blood thinned to perfection — unplugged. Reborn — the cord was cut. Julia collected — we walked under the night sky. First stop, The Wheel at Tresillian.

"You're the chap in the Mirror dinghy." (I landed in their beer garden two and a half years before.)

"I carried on, round Land's End last summer . . . and hope to continue voyaging when the days are longer. A medium white and pint of mild please?"

David Weston, Mevagissey.

January 1995.

EPIC

El cielo nocturno

Kimberly M. Hutmacher

Editor del contenido científico:
Shirley Duke

rourkeeducationalmedia.com

Teacher Notes available at
rem4teachers.com

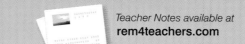

Science Content Editor: Shirley Duke holds a bachelor's degree in biology and a master's degree in education from Austin College in Sherman, Texas. She taught science in Texas at all levels for twenty-five years before starting to write for children. Her science books include *You Can't Wear These Genes, Infections, Infestations, and Diseases, Enterprise STEM, Forces and Motion at Work, Environmental Disasters,* and *Gases*. She continues writing science books and also works as a science content editor.

www.rourkeeducationalmedia.com

Photo credits: Cover © Orla, Igor Kovalchuk, Snaprender; Pages 2/3 © jupeart; Pages 4/5 © sebikus; Pages 6/7 © Andrew F. Kazmierski, pjmorley; Pages 8/9 © godrick, Viktar Malyshchyts, Bob Orsillo; Pages 10/11 © Primož Cigler, oorka; Pages 12/13 © NASA, Giovanni Benintende; Pages 14/15 © courtesy of ESO astronomer Yuri Beletsky, jupeart, olly; Pages 16/17 © NASA, silver tiger; Pages 18/19 © shooarts, ella1977; Pages 20/21 © Kostyantyn Ivanyshen, Mark R

Editor: Kelli Hicks

My Science Library series produced by Blue Door Publishing, Florida for Rourke Educational Media.
Editorial/Production Services in Spanish
by Cambridge BrickHouse, Inc.
www.cambridgebh.com

Hutmacher, Kimberly M.
El cielo nocturno / Kimberly M. Hutmacher.
(Mi biblioteca de ciencia)
ISBN 978-1-63155-047-8 (hard cover - Spanish)
ISBN 978-1-62717-340-7 (soft cover - Spanish)
ISBN 978-1-62717-547-0 (e-Book - Spanish)
ISBN 978-1-61810-225-6 (soft cover-English)
Library of Congress Control Number: 2014941467

Also Available as:

Rourke Educational Media
Printed in the United States of America,
North Mankato, Minnesota

rourkeeducationalmedia.com
customerservice@rourkeeducationalmedia.com
PO Box 643328 Vero Beach, Florida 32964

Contenido

Sol

¡Hola, vecino!

El vecino más cercano de la Tierra en el espacio es la Luna. La Tierra orbita alrededor del Sol y la Luna orbita alrededor de la Tierra. ¿Sabías que la Luna no tiene luz propia? El brillo de la Luna proviene de la luz solar cuando se refleja sobre su superficie.

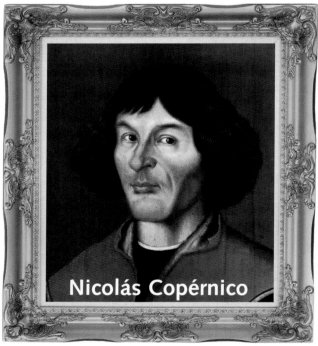

Nicolás Copérnico

En el pasado se pensaba que la Tierra era el centro del sistema solar. En 1543, Nicolás Copérnico publicó una teoría revolucionaria que ponía al Sol en el centro del sistema solar.

Los **atrónomos** son científicos que estudian el universo. Ellos piensan que la Luna formaba parte de la Tierra. Hace billones de años un objeto proveniente del espacio chocó contra la Tierra y le arrancó pedazos grandes. Los científicos creen que esos pedazos se juntaron y se endurecieron, formando la Luna.

Luna

Tierra

Las caras de la Luna

Cuando observamos la Luna durante un mes, parece cambiar de forma. En realidad, la Luna no cambia de forma, solo parece cambiar porque solo podemos ver las partes iluminadas por el Sol. La Luna nos muestra siempre la misma cara. Mientras orbita, vemos distintas formas, llamadas **fases lunares**.

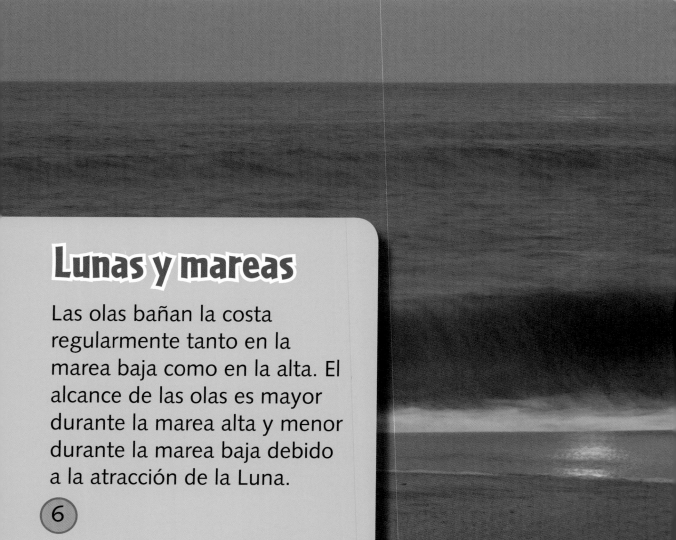

Lunas y mareas

Las olas bañan la costa regularmente tanto en la marea baja como en la alta. El alcance de las olas es mayor durante la marea alta y menor durante la marea baja debido a la atracción de la Luna.

Cada semana del mes, la Luna recorre un cuarto de su órbita alrededor de la Tierra. Cuando la Tierra pasa entre la Luna y el Sol y la cara iluminada de la Luna está frente a la Tierra, podemos ver la Luna llena.

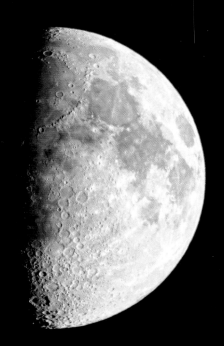

Una semana después solo podemos ver la mitad de su luz reflejada.

Otra semana después solo podemos ver una lasca iluminada de la Luna en forma creciente.

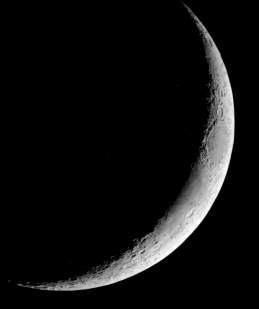

La cuarta semana vemos la Luna nueva. La Luna pasa entre el Sol y la Tierra y el Sol ilumina la cara oculta de la Luna. Pareciera como si la Luna hubiese desaparecido, pero sigue ahí, solo que no podemos verla.

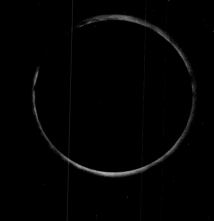

La Tierra solo tiene una luna, pero más de ciento cuarenta lunas han sido descubiertas orbitando los planetas de nuestro **sistema solar.**

Proyectando sombras

Durante un **eclipse lunar**, la Luna pasa detrás de la Tierra, y la Tierra bloquea el paso de la luz solar. Esto a veces proyecta una sombra en la Luna.

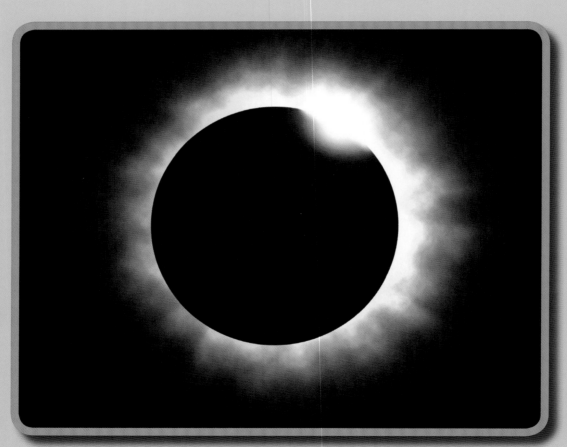

Un eclipse solar ocurre cuando la Luna pasa entre el Sol y la Tierra y la sombra de la Luna es proyectada en la Tierra.

Esta fotografía muestra un eclipse lunar ocurrido en 2007. Los eclipses lunares ocurren de dos a cuatro veces al año.

Polvo, rocas y nieve

Los **asteroides** son rocas espaciales que orbitan alrededor del Sol. El Gran Cinturón está formado por billones de asteroides. Cada asteroide se demora de tres a seis años en completar una órbita alrededor del Sol.

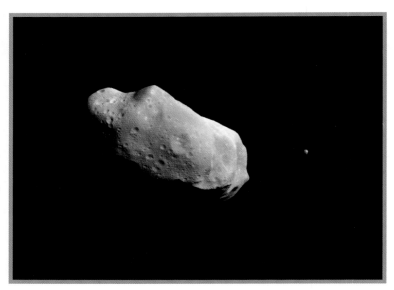

Casi todos los asteroides de nuestro sistema solar están localizados en el Cinturón de Asteroides ubicado entre las órbitas de Marte y Júpiter.

cometa

Un **cometa** es un cuerpo espacial pequeño hecho de nieve, hielo y polvo. También se le llama bola de nieve sucia. Un **meteoroide** es un pequeño pedazo de cometa o asteroide. La luz que provoca un meteoroide al pasar por nuestra atmósfera es llamada **meteoro** o estrella fugaz.

Nace una estrella

Nuestro cielo nocturno está iluminado por billones de estrellas. Las estrellas son bolas gigantes de gas caliente y resplandeciente que brillan en nuestro universo. El Sol no es la estrella más brillante, pero parece serlo porque es la más cercana a la Tierra. Todas las estrellas de nuestra **galaxia** pertenecen a un grupo llamado la Vía Láctea. Se llaman así porque todas unidas parecen un camino hecho de leche.

Vía Láctea

Hay estrellas de muchos tamaños. Algunas son 100 o 200
veces más grandes que el Sol y otras son más pequeñas
que la Tierra.

Los científicos usan
un telescopio para
observar el
cielo nocturno.

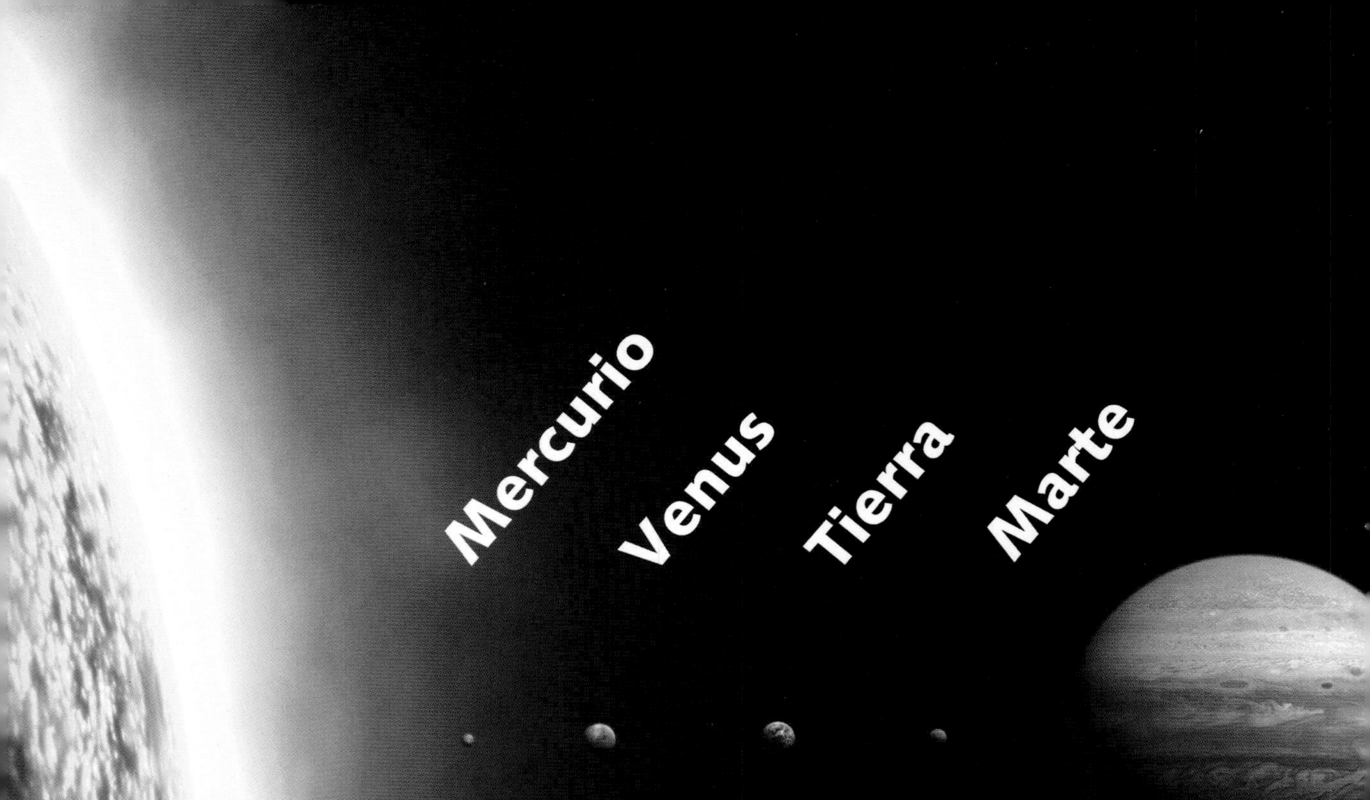

Mercurio

Venus

Tierra

Marte

El Sol

Los planetas dan vueltas alrededor de una estrella y obtienen luz de la estrella a medida que orbitan alrededor de esta. La Tierra orbita alrededor del Sol, una estrella de mediano tamaño. La Tierra rota hacia el Este, por lo que el Sol sale por el Este y se pone por el Oeste.

Nuestro sistema solar está compuesto por todos los planetas que orbitan alrededor del Sol, todas las lunas, cometas, asteroides, planetas menores más pequeños, polvo y gas.

Saturno

Urano

Neptuno

A la Tierra le toma un año entero completar una órbita alrededor del Sol.

Dibujos estelares

Hace mucho tiempo, las personas notaron que ciertas estrellas agrupadas formaban dibujos de personas, animales y objetos, en el firmamento. Estos dibujos son llamados **constelaciones** y los antiguos romanos les dieron nombres.

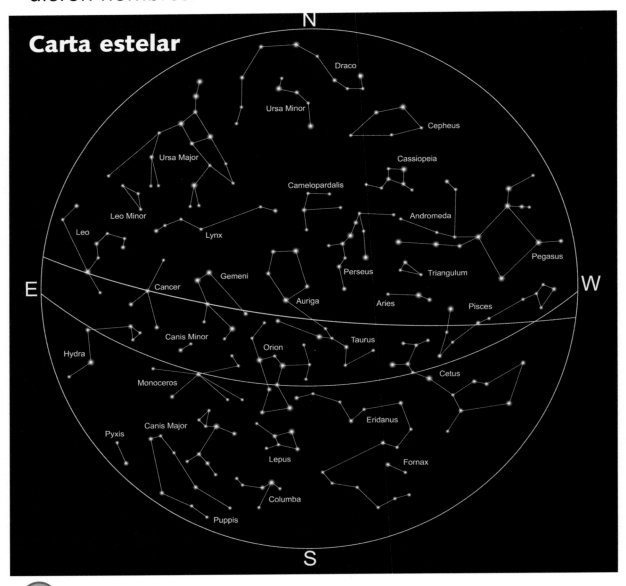

Carta estelar

N

Draco

Ursa Minor

Cepheus

Ursa Major

Cassiopeia

Camelopardalis

Andromeda

Leo Minor

Pegasus

Leo

Lynx

Perseus

Triangulum

Gemeni

Cancer

Auriga

Aries

Pisces

E

W

Canis Minor

Taurus

Hydra

Orion

Monoceros

Cetus

Canis Major

Eridanus

Pyxis

Lepus

Fornax

Columba

Puppis

S

Los astrónomos hacen cartas estelares. Las cartas estelares son mapas del cielo nocturno que podemos usar para encontrar constelaciones.

La Osa Mayor está en la constelación *Ursa Major* y la Osa Menor, también llamada *Ursa Minor*, parece un carro de tiro. La estrella al final del mango del carro se llama Estrella Polar o Estrella del Norte.

Estrella Polar (del Norte)

La Osa Menor (Ursa Minor)

Orión parece un cazador con un garrote, un escudo y un cinturón. Cerca de Orión podemos ver la constelación Canis Major, también conocida como Can Mayor o Perro grande.

Orión

Can Mayor

Las estrellas han ayudado a la humanidad por miles de años. Nos han ayudado a **navegar** a donde hemos querido ir y a llevar la cuenta del tiempo. ¡El cielo nocturno no es solo hermoso, sino también muy últil!

Demuestra lo que sabes

1. ¿Tiene la Luna luz propia? Si no tiene, ¿de dónde viene?

2. ¿Cuáles son los nombres de dos constelaciones descritas en este libro?

3. ¿Qué hace un astrónomo?

Glosario

asteroides: rocas espaciales que orbitan alrededor del Sol

astrónomos: científicos que estudian el universo y todo lo que contiene

cometa: objeto celeste pequeño hecho de nieve, hielo y polvo

constelaciones: estrellas que, agrupadas, forman un dibujo

galaxia: grupo grande de estrellas, gas y polvo que permanecen juntos debido a la acción de la fuerza de gravedad

eclipse lunar: bloqueo parcial o total de la luz proveniente de la Luna ocasionado por la Tierra cuando pasa entre el Sol y la Luna, proyectando su sombra sobre la Luna

fases lunares: las distintas partes iluminadas de la Luna que se ven durante el transcurso del mes

meteoro: luz provocada cuando un meteoroide pasa por la atmósfera de la Tierra

meteoroide: pedazo de un cometa o asteroide

navegar: llevar un barco o un avión por un camino planeado

sistema solar: el Sol, los planetas y todo lo que orbita alrededor del Sol

Índice

Sitios de la internet

www.nasa.gov/audience/forstudents/k-4/finditfast/K-8_Topical_Index.
   html#c

www.loc.gov/rr/scitech/mysteries/bluemoon.html

http://science.nationalgeographic.com/science/space/solar-system/

Sobre la autora

Kimberly M. Hutmacher es la autora de 24 libros para niños. A ella le encanta investigar temas relacionados con las ciencias y compartir lo que aprende. También disfruta compartir su amor por la escritura con audiencias de todas las edades.

¡Pregúntale a la autora!
www.rem4students.com